PRAISE FOR THE NEGOTIATION BOOK

"The go-to book on negotiation. Discover how to deal with negotiating gameplay so you can have confident commercial conversations whatever the situation."

Colin Hutchinson, Chief Operating Officer, Edgewell Personal Care

"After reading *The Negotiation Book*, I can now say I've learned everything I need to know to help me master the art of negotiation!"

Major General Jonathan Shaw, Chairman, Optima

"If you want to become a world-class negotiator, I strongly suggest you read this book. You'll learn how to harness your EQ to truly understand what makes you and the other party tick so you can successfully negotiate a win-win outcome."

James Arnold, Head of Corporate Treasury, Investec Bank

"An easy and engaging read packed with expert advice designed to help you take your negotiation skills to the next level. Nicole has a very straightforward and clear way of laying out the art of negotiation and the necessity of learning how to navigate important conversations."

Matthew Serynek, Managing Director, IHS Markit

"Easy to understand and full of everyday scenarios that bring negotiation theory to life, *The Negotiation Book*'s step-by-step approach to developing your negotiation skills is an inspiring read."

Mandy Ferguson, VP, Harlequin

Published by
LID Publishing Ltd
The Record Hall, Studio 204,
16-16a Baldwins Gardens,
London EC1N 7RJ, UK

524 Broadway, 11th Floor, Suite 08-120,
New York, NY 10012, US

info@lidpublishing.com
www.lidpublishing.com

A member of:
BPR
Business Publishers Roundtable

www.businesspublishersroundtable.com

© Nicole Soames, 2017
© LID Publishing Ltd, 2017
Reprinted 2017, 2018

Printed in Latvia by Jelgavas Tipogrāfija

ISBN: 978-1-911498-42-1

Cover and page design: Caroline Li

THE NEGOTIATION BOOK

PRACTICAL STEPS
TO BECOMING A MASTER NEGOTIATOR

NICOLE SOAMES

LONDON   NEW YORK   BOGOTA
MADRID   BARCELONA   BUENOS AIRES
MEXICO CITY   MONTERREY   SAN FRANCISCO
SHANGHAI

FOR OTHER TITLES
IN THE SERIES...

CONCISE
ADVICE
LAB

SMALL BOOKS: BIG IDEAS

CLEVER CONTENT, DYNAMIC IDEAS, PRACTICAL
SOLUTIONS AND ENGAGING VISUALS –
A CATALYST TO INSPIRE NEW WAYS OF THINKING
AND PROBLEM-SOLVING IN A COMPLEX WORLD

conciseadvicelab.com

CONTENTS

INTRODUCTION

"When was the last time you negotiated?"
As CEO of a commercial skills training and coaching company who has helped thousands of people all over the world master the art of negotiation, I am always surprised by the responses I get to this question. In the majority of cases, people name the last time they were involved in a major personal purchase such as buying a new car or a house. In their mind negotiation is associated with money and buying or selling something.

In reality, we negotiate all the time. Whether it is negotiating with our family or friends over whose turn it is to drive on a night out, or agreeing the scope of a project with your colleagues or customers – negotiation happens on a daily basis. The great news is that negotiation, just like any other life skill, can be learned and developed over time and this book is designed to help you do just that. Packed with practical advice, expert tools and techniques and commercial know-how, *The Negotiation Book* will give you the skills and confidence to help you become a master negotiator.

1. WHAT IS NEGOTIATION?
All too often, people mistakenly assume that negotiation is a form of argument that results in one party or the other getting their own

way. In people's minds, negotiation is synonymous with bartering or haggling or, in extreme cases, complex legal wranglings and hostage talks. However, this combative understanding of negotiation overlooks the fact that negotiating is a communication skill that should be an integral part of any commercial toolkit.

So, what exactly do we mean by negotiation?

I define negotiation as, **"Communication between two parties to find overlapping positions. When conducted and concluded masterfully this ends with at least one party 'winning' and one party 'compromising'."**

This definition clearly shows the important role communication plays in negotiating successfully. Negotiation should be, by its very nature, a two-way conversation that enables you to find common ground. An easier way to explain this is to look at the graph below.

In this scenario, the seller is trying to put the price up and the buyer is trying to lower it. The area in the middle is the negotiation zone. This is the win zone – a position that is amenable to both parties.

I often describe negotiation as the ritual dance that helps you to identify this win zone – it can be done with two left feet or it can be done flawlessly. Negotiations can easily go wrong when people allow the relationship in question to cloud their judgment. More often than not, novice negotiators end up conceding because they perceive negotiation to be a confrontation. Master negotiators, on the other hand, work hard to manage the negotiation conversations to find an outcome that benefits both parties.

2. WHEN SHOULD YOU NEGOTIATE?

In my experience, people often confuse negotiation with selling and, consequently, start negotiating too early. For example, if you have a rolling contract with a customer, you should try to influence their decision by selling them the benefits before you start negotiating the deal. Negotiations should only begin once one party has set out their stall and actually made a proposal. This is the pivotal moment when you realize the selling has been completed and you need to start negotiating in order to reach closure.

The ability to switch from selling to negotiating can be easier said than done. In reality, in business you do not attend 'sales' or 'nego-tiation' meetings, just 'meetings'. You therefore need to have the presence of mind to read the situation and switch to a negotiation mindset so that you can control the outcome. To help you achieve this, this book will provide a framework that you can replicate to practise good negotiations.

3. HOW EMOTIONAL INTELLIGENCE CAN HELP YOU NEGOTIATE

Whenever I deliver negotiation workshops, I start by asking everyone who they think is the toughest negotiator in the room. Invariably, they say that I must be as I am the negotiation expert. And I always tell them that the toughest person to negotiate with is yourself.

As human beings, we are often our own worst enemies. We talk ourselves down before we even get to the negotiating table. There's no denying that being able to manage and control your emotions is a key factor in achieving negotiation success. This approach is in stark contrast to the negotiation training I received when I started my career more than 25 years ago. Most negotiation theories advise you to take any emotion out of the equation by viewing negotiation as a process. The focus of this training is always about the other party, with very little time given to managing your own feelings.

My eureka moment came when I was introduced to the power of emotional intelligence (EQ) by fellow author in this series, Dr Martyn Newman. He described EQ as "a set of emotional and social skills that are most effective at influencing others."

I quickly recognized that being able to draw on your EQ skills was crucial to negotiating effectively. If you refer back to my definition of negotiation as the "communication between two parties to find overlapping positions," it is clear that the ability to use your EQ skills to influence the other party will enable you to secure the best possible outcome. Master negotiators, therefore, need to draw on their social skills, self-awareness, self-management and ambition to build a relationship with the other party that enables them to find an overlapping position. After all, it is important to remember that people like doing business with people they like. In the following chapters I will show you exactly how to harness your different EQ skills so you can master the art of negotiation.

4. YOUR JOURNEY TO BECOMING A MASTER NEGOTIATOR

It takes commitment, ambition and practise to hone your negotiation skills and unlock your commercial confidence to become a master negotiator. To help you on your journey, I have broken down the process into steps with easy-to-manage bite-sized explanations. I have based the steps on real-life scenarios I have experienced during my 25 years of commercial experience combined with over 12 years of developing and delivering negotiation training and coaching internationally in a diverse range of sectors.

I have not reinvented the wheel – some of what I cover, you may already be doing intuitively. However, the focus throughout is on how to develop your EQ to help you on your way, and, although often described as soft skills, they are often the hardest skills to master in life. For this reason, I have worked hard to make the difficult stuff accessible.

I am well aware that all too many negotiation books get left untouched on the bookshelf. So, in keeping with the rest of the concise advice series, I have designed *The Negotiation Book* to be used in a practical way on a regular basis. Each of the following chapters contain easy-to-use tools and techniques combined with expert advice to help you put the negotiation theory into practice. I do not believe in a text book approach to learning, so please try and use this book as a workbook – scribble notes in the margins, fill out the exercises, and keep referring back to the key takeaways at the end of each chapter to help you embed your learning. After all, as Benjamin Franklin said, *"Tell me and I forget, teach me and I may remember, involve me and I learn."*

PART ONE

DEVELOPING
A NEGOTIATING
MINDSET

The first step on your journey to becoming a master negotiator is to develop a winning mindset. The ability to get your mind in the right space before you begin to negotiate is critical to your overall success. I am often reminded of Henry Ford's wise words: *"**Whether you think you can or think you can't – you are right.**"* This is especially true in the case of negotiation. As human beings we are disproportionately more likely to focus on the negatives than positives, which means we can spend more time negotiating with ourselves than with anyone else. So how do you make sure that you silence those negative voices in your head (which are often the loudest) and think **'you can'** instead?

WHAT IS A WINNING MINDSET?

Without doubt, one of the most iconic examples of the power of a winning mindset is seeing the New Zealand All Blacks perform the haka. No one can fail to be impressed by the way it galvanizes the team, boosting their confidence and preparing them for the match ahead. The haka originated as an ancestral war dance, but it has evolved to be more than a way of intimidating counterparts on the pitch. It is used by the players to get their heads in the right zone before they kick the ball. The sheer physicality of the haka also reminds us of the important role body language plays in unlocking our confidence. Now, I am not suggesting you start doing a war cry before your next negotiation, but there are lessons you can learn from the haka about how to prepare both mentally and physically so you enter negotiations feeling at the top of your game.

THE IMPORTANCE OF SELF-AWARENESS

Before you begin looking at practical steps to develop your negotiating mindset, it is important to take a few moments to understand the role that self-awareness plays in your personal development. As Aristotle remarked, **"Knowing yourself is the beginning of all wisdom."** Self-awareness is your ability to understand and recognize your emotions and the effect they have on others. It is only by developing emotional awareness that you can identify your personal strengths and areas for development.

FOUR WAYS TO BECOME MORE SELF-AWARE:

1. **Be mindful** – being present and focusing on the moment will help develop your self-awareness.

2. **Take a personality profiling test** – such as DISC or Myers-Briggs to gain a clearer understanding of your communication style and those of others.

3. **Ask for feedback** – both formal and informal, at work or from trusted friends.

4. **Write down your priorities and ambitions** – take the time to identify your key motivators and drivers.

1. STEPPING OUT OF YOUR COMFORT ZONE

Once you've taken the time to understand what really makes you tick, you can use this awareness to help develop your negotiation skills. Remember, what doesn't challenge you doesn't change you! This is true whether you are learning a new language, training for a marathon or starting to play a musical instrument – and is especially the case if you want to become a master negotiator.

This desire for self-improvement is what differentiates successful people; they constantly challenge the status quo so they can achieve the extraordinary. The great news is that everyone can take practical steps to develop a winning mindset – it takes ambition, commitment and hard work.

The graph highlights the important role challenge plays in driving your negotiation performance. The vertical axis shows your level of performance, and the horizontal axis represents how much you are challenging yourself. The graph clearly shows that people perform at their best when they experience a medium level of challenge by moving out of their comfort zone into their stretch zone. This is the area of best performance. However, if you challenge yourself even further, you risk entering your panic zone. Here your performance levels dip once again.

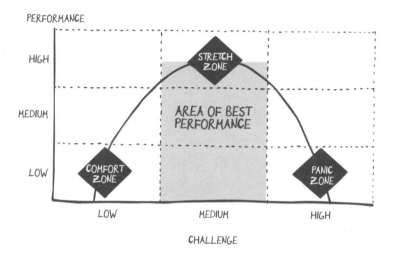

PERFORMANCE

HIGH

MEDIUM

LOW

STRETCH ZONE

AREA OF BEST PERFORMANCE

COMFORT ZONE

PANIC ZONE

LOW   MEDIUM   HIGH

CHALLENGE

Moving out of your comfort zone can often be easier said than done. It is called a comfort zone for a reason – it is the mental space in which you feel emotionally secure. This is not always a bad thing, as it can protect you by helping you feel cosy and safe. However, it can also lead to negative emotions. It can cause you to shy away from negotiating opportunities rather than tackle them head on. You may also become complacent and think you no longer need to prepare for negotiations because you've been there before.

In either scenario, staying in your comfort zone will eventually prevent you from achieving the best negotiating outcome. It is only by pushing the limits and moving into your stretch zone that you will learn and develop. This ability to constantly raise the bar is what differentiates master negotiators. By adopting this winning mindset, you will always challenge yourself to be in the best negotiating position.

FIVE SIGNS YOU ARE STUCK AT THE BOTTOM OF YOUR COMFORT ZONE:

1. You feel bored.
2. You are self-critical.
3. You feel demotivated.
4. You have low self-esteem.
5. You are easily distracted.

MOVING INTO YOUR STRETCH ZONE

Your stretch zone is where the magic happens. It could be negotiating a large contract with a new client, or negotiating a pay rise with your boss. These are scenarios which push you outside your comfort zone but do not have you running for the hills in panic.

I can clearly remember one particular occasion as a young account manager when I had been asked to negotiate an unjustifiable price increase. I felt well and truly outside of my comfort zone, so I talked the situation through with my senior colleagues and they reassured me that the other party needed our products as much as we needed the price increase. This gave me the boost I needed to draw on my reserves of courage and go to the negotiation table. The experience made me understand just how much preparation I needed to do to negotiate successfully. This, in turn, helped unlock my commercial confidence when it came to future negotiations.

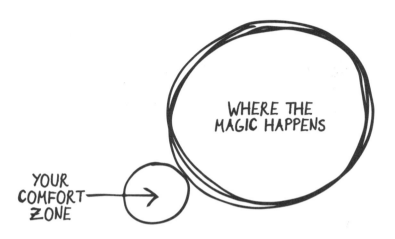

WHERE THE
MAGIC HAPPENS

YOUR
COMFORT
ZONE

SIX STEPS TO MOVE INTO YOUR STRETCH ZONE:

1. **Face Your Fears** – write a list of your main concerns, e.g. "They are never going to agree to my terms," and then think of a counter argument.

2. **Make a plan** – think about all the various negotiating scenarios and the different outcomes the negotiations may deliver.

3. **Find support** – find a mentor, coach, or colleague to brainstorm ideas and scenarios.

4. **Visualize success** – imagine yourself signing your name on the contract.

5. **Break the negotiation into bite-sized chunks** – remember, you do not need to do it all in one go.

6. **Be inspired by others** – who do you know who is a master negotiator? Ask yourself what they would do in this situation.

Finally, one word of caution: while moving into your stretch zone will help you reap the rewards of greater confidence and increase results, a move into your panic zone can have the opposite effect. Feeling stressed and completely out of your depth will undermine your confidence and reduce the likeliness of you achieving your desired result.

FIVE SIGNS THAT YOU ARE IN YOUR PANIC ZONE:

1. You feel overwhelmed and cannot think straight.
2. You find it difficult to make a decision.
3. You cannot sleep properly or wake up worrying.
4. You suffer from tension headaches or stomach troubles.
5. Constructive feedback feels like personal criticism.

2. BALANCING THE PLAYING FIELD

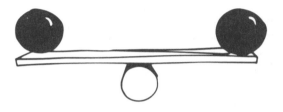

The balance of power lies at the heart of negotiation. Interestingly, based on more than 25 years of negotiation experience, I have noticed that, in the majority of cases, people presume the other party has the balance of power. The more you want something, the more this becomes true. So, in emotionally charged negotiations such as for a job or a house, you are far more likely to believe you are on the back foot, which weakens your negotiating position.

Master negotiators, on the other hand, understand that the secret to negotiation success is balancing the playing field. The best negotiations are those that are mutually beneficial and allow both parties to leave the table feeling they have got something out of the deal.

TAKE CARE WITH RELATIONSHIPS

In many negotiation scenarios, the perceived balance of power is different from the reality. All too often people end up 'paying' for their relationships because they mistakenly think the other party holds all the cards. This is particularly true when negotiating internally or with family – in both cases the other party knows exactly what makes you tick and where you are weak. They may be tempted to leverage this against you.

For example, if you are negotiating your package for a new job with your would-be employer, it can be easy to adopt a master-servant relationship in which you feel they have all the power. Whereas, in reality, you are equally important because they need something you have. So be balanced and remember you do not have to say yes to all their terms and conditions. Try to put yourself in the other person's shoes by asking yourself how it makes you feel when someone is subservient to you? Usually people say they feel sorry for that person or secretly hope to take advantage of them. In either case, this will weaken your negotiating position.

Whatever your role, remember to avoid a master–servant relationship. If you treat someone like a servant, they are more likely to act in that way. If you appear arrogant, they will want to take you down a peg or two or avoid having to deal with you by finding a route around you. If they do give in to your demands, they can feel like they have been taken for a ride, which may sour the relationship in the long term.

However, if you enter negotiations in a balanced way, feeling like an equal, you are more likely to build a relationship based on trust and respect that will deliver success for both parties over the long term.

HOW TO CREATE A LEVEL PLAYING FIELD

Before you enter negotiations, ask yourself how you can feel equal. Re-balance things in your head by identifying exactly what you bring to the table. For example, as an account manager, whenever

I was negotiating with a client, I would reverse the roles in my head and tell myself that they needed to convince me why I should invest in their routes to our consumers. By remembering that the clients needed our products and investment, it balanced the playing field in my mind, which helped me feel more confident during the negotiations.

Finally, remember you do not need to negotiate in every case. If you feel that the relationship can't be balanced, take the time to decide if you are in or out. Remind yourself that you are there to win the war, not just to fight the battle.

3. SILENCING YOUR INNER GREMLINS

As I mentioned at the beginning of this chapter, when it comes to negotiation we often have more battles with ourselves than with anyone else. As we enter a negotiating situation, tension starts to rise and the voices inside our head, those negotiating inner gremlins, can all too easily take hold and undermine the balance of power.

In cases such as this, my advice is always to turn the volume down. Chances are you may have been personally involved with the initial sale, so are very keen to conclude the negotiations as quickly as possible. The more we want something, the easier it is for those negotiating demons to shout loudly in your ears: "I know this is going to end in negotiation deadlock."

Silence those negative thoughts by focusing on what is brilliant about your company, your sector and, finally, your relationship with your client. By focusing on the positive you will enter the negotiations with a winning mindset and stand a higher chance of achieving the result you want.

The table is a handy tool to help you establish a winning mindset, so remember to take the time to fill it in before you start negotiating.

Begin at the macro level and write down what is great about the company you work for, then drill down by focusing on why you should feel confident about your specific division, the relationship you have with your counterpart and, finally, your own personal strengths and skills. By putting pen to paper in this way, you will immediately boost your confidence so that you enter the negotiations on the front foot.

WINNING MINDSET	WHY SHOULD I FEEL CONFIDENT ABOUT...
THIS COMPANY	
THIS DIVISION	
THIS CUSTOMER	
MYSELF	

4. SEEING THE GLASS HALF FULL

The ability to focus on the positives of a situation is crucial to mastering the art of negotiation. Optimistic people are more likely to be solution-orientated and this helps keep the negotiation moving forward. As Winston Churchill said, *"A pessimist sees the difficulty in every opportunity; the optimist sees the opportunity in every difficulty."*

As humans, we are hardwired to be more negative than positive. There is an evolutionary basis for this: it helps us to survive threats and manage risk. However, it also means that when circumstances do not turn out like we had hoped, it is easy to fall into a downward spiral of negative thoughts. In extreme cases, people start catastrophizing by imagining worst-case scenarios.

Emotionally resilient people, on the other hand, have the ability to reframe negative thoughts into positive ones. This doesn't just mean flipping negatives into their opposite – instead, it is about being realistically optimistic. For example, if you are worried that your negotiations may end in deadlock, be an optimistic person and think, "What other variables can I bring to the table to keep the negotiations moving?" By avoiding black-and-white thinking and finding shades of grey, you will see the positives in a situation and achieve your desired outcome.

FIVE WAYS TO REWIRE YOUR BRAIN TO BECOME MORE OPTIMISTIC:

1. **Turn negatives into positives** – boost your self-belief by silencing your inner chatter. Instead of believing, "it is going to be impossible to push back on their demands," tell yourself, "I have the skills and experience to influence the outcome and this is how I am going to do it."

2. **Do not be a perfectionist** – give yourself permission to make mistakes now and again. Try not to judge yourself harder than you judge others. When someone gives you a compliment, accept it graciously.

3. **Be proud** – own your successes. Do not put them down to luck or being in the right place at the right time. Being proud of yourself, your team and your work are powerful ingredients that drive success. By picturing what looks good, you are more likely to develop a winning mindset that sets you apart from the competition.

4. **Use positive body language** – just as it is difficult to say something negative with a smile on your face, the opposite is also true. To build a winning mindset, your body language, tone of voice, and inner chatter all need to be positive.

5. **Believe in your abilities** – we can all be plagued with self-doubt at one time or another. Whenever you feel your self-esteem is taking a tumble, write a list of your key skills and strengths. Find evidence of when you successfully turned around negotiations that seemed impossible at the time; this can help boost your confidence levels and strengthen your negotiating position.

It is important to be optimistic before, during and after negotiations. Negotiations can often be protracted and complicated – initial optimism can soon give way to frustration and negativity when things do not turn out as you had planned. Master negotiators understand the importance of taking the learnings and moving on – using their creativity to find another solution. Remember, it is not over until the fat lady sings!

KEY TAKEAWAYS

You should now be in no doubt about the importance of getting your head in the right place before you begin negotiating.

The secret to developing a winning mindset is to:

- Take the time to understand what really makes you tick so you can identify your negotiating strengths and areas for development.
- Keep raising the bar – remember what does not challenge you does not change you.
- Have the ambition and drive to move from your comfort zone into your stretch zone (but resist falling into your panic zone).
- Before you enter negotiations, rebalance things in your mind – do not be tempted to pay for your relationships.
- Do not negotiate with yourself – silence your inner chatter and focus on what is good about you, your work and your company.
- Be realistically optimistic – turn negatives into positives and believe in your ability to negotiate successfully.

PART TWO

PREPARING FOR NEGOTIATING SUCCESS

People mistakenly think the best negotiators are those who think quickly on their feet. Whereas, in reality, the most successful negotiators are those that are well prepared. As Benjamin Franklin so wisely said, *"If you are failing to prepare, you are preparing to fail."* However, you would be amazed how many people do fail to prepare effectively and think, instead, that they can wing it. In fact, the art of appearing like a born negotiator is to prepare so well behind the scenes that it looks like you are thinking live and in the moment.

Based on my extensive experience delivering negotiation training, I have found that the main reason people fall at this hurdle is that they do not know *what* they should prepare. So, the second stage on your journey to becoming a master negotiator is to recognize that preparation is crucial to negotiation success, and to learn how to do it well.

WHEN SHOULD YOU PREPARE FOR NEGOTIATIONS?

The answer is all the time. People often go into a meeting unaware that they will end up negotiating, so you always need to be prepared just in case, or you risk being negotiated 'at'. The other mistake people often make is thinking they only need to prepare for large formal negotiations. In fact, you need to take even more time to prepare for negotiations in which you are emotionally involved, such as negotiating the price of your new home or asking your boss for a pay rise.

And this does not just mean jotting down a few notes five minutes before you sit at the negotiating table. You should prepare before, at the start, during, in your win zone, and after your negotiations.

The more you prepare, the more creative you will be and the more options you can bring to the negotiations. By breaking down your preparation into bite-sized chunks in this way, you will have the tools in your kitbag to keep the negotiations moving forwards. (But more about this when I show you how to make your negotiation proposal in Part Five.)

WHAT SHOULD YOU PREPARE?

Having established that preparation is king, the area that people really struggle with is understanding exactly what they should prepare. Most people focus on the commercial aspects of the negotiation and spend their time preparing figures. However, the risk in doing this is that you may overlook the preparation of the more intangible but all-important aspects of negotiation.

To gain a clearer understanding of what you should be preparing, remind yourself of the definition of negotiation given in the introduction: "Communication between two parties to find overlapping positions." This is where your EQ needs to come to the forefront; it is only by identifying and understanding your own motivators and those of your counterpart's that you can discover an overlapping position that will result in a successful negotiation.

1. UNDERSTANDING YOUR OWN NEGOTIATION STYLE

When I started my career, nearly every negotiation course I went on focused on the other party and gave scant attention to the role we, as individuals, play in negotiations. This startling oversight fails to take into account that it really does take two to tango. In fact, the first step in preparing for any negotiations is self-knowledge, as only then will you be able to identify the overlapping position between you and the other party.

It is only by understanding your own particular needs that you can prepare effectively for the different negotiation scenarios you may face. A good way to achieve this is by using the '5 whys' principle – start by asking what outcome you want from this particular negotiation, then drill down by asking yourself 'why' and 'why' again until you have got to the root of the issue. Remember, unless you know exactly what you plan to gain from the negotiations, you are unlikely to get the negotiation outcome you need.

USE YOUR EQ TO UNCOVER YOUR NEGOTIATING SELF

As we said earlier, self-awareness is the cornerstone of EQ – so take the time to understand exactly what makes you tick and the effect this has on the other party before, during and after the negotiation. By harnessing your EQ in this way, you will begin to understand exactly what pushes your buttons and the behaviour this creates. For example, if your counterpart acts in a bullish and direct manner, you may feel irritated, which can negatively affect your decision-making process and weaken your negotiating position. By identifying these triggers and their effect on you, you are more likely to stay in control and influence the outcome of the negotiations.

HOW TO IDENTIFY YOUR DOMINANT NEGOTIATING STYLE

We are all a blend of different negotiating styles, however, you will generally have a style that you default to. This is particularly true when you feel under pressure, as you are more likely to behave in a certain way. It is important to remember that there is no better or worse negotiating style – you just need to understand which is your most dominant one.

Broadly speaking there are four different negotiating styles:
1. Confident and results driven.
2. Outgoing and persuasive.
3. Dependable and consistent.
4. Detail orientated and outcome focused.

Use the statements on the next page to help you identify your most dominant style. You may find that you tick a range of comments so choose the negotiating style that is the most applicable to you. Remember, it should reflect your authentic self, and not the person you would like to be. So, try to be honest and objective about how you respond to different negotiating situations.

CONFIDENT AND RESULTS DRIVEN	OUTGOING AND PERSUASIVE	DEPENDABLE AND CONSISTENT	DETAIL ORIENTATED AND OUTCOME FOCUSED
I am competitive	I prefer to think of the bigger picture rather than get bogged down in the analytical details	I am concerned about what is going on for them	The results are more important than the relationship
I focus on the result, not the relationship		I am a good listener and consider their positions, too	I am analytical and must know the detail before we start
They will respect me if I go in hard	Relationships are key when negotiating	I am happy if they get what they want	I do not like surprises
I will keep going until I get what I want	I am often thinking about the impact on the relationship	I do not like confrontation	I never show emotion when negotiating
I will do what I can to win and get the best result	I do not want them to think badly of me	I like negotiations to be calm and not get heated	If it doesn't work for me I will walk and not worry about the relationship
I am happy making the decisions	I do not want to rock the boat	I do not like to rush decisions	
I like to be in control	I cannot help but show emotions when negotiating	If I feel intimidated or it gets tough I tend to retreat	I do not like to rush decisions, I would rather withdraw than be pushed
The quicker the better			

Once you have identified your negotiating style, use this information to help you understand how this will affect your behaviour before, during and after your negotiations.

2. PUTTING YOURSELF IN THE OTHER PARTY'S SHOES

"Three quarters of the miseries and misunderstandings in the world would finish if people were to put on the shoes of their adversaries and understood their points of view." Mahatma Gandhi

Having gained a deeper knowledge of yourself, you now need to continue your preparation by understanding your counterpart's particular needs and challenges.

It is only by understanding what truly motivates them – both commercially and personally – that you can hope to influence them. By putting yourself in the other party's shoes, you should be able to identify any hidden issues that may block negotiations down the road. Remember, the best negotiations benefit both parties, so it is vital that you continue to remind yourself of their needs as part of your preparation.

In Stephen Covey's seminal book, *The 7 Habits of Highly Effective People*, habit number five is "Seek first to understand, then to be understood". This is often easier said than done – in a meeting, more often than not most of us are so keen to get our own point of view across that we do not take the time to understand the other person's perspective. The majority of people do not anticipate what the other may be thinking because they get so wrapped up in planning what they want to achieve. In fact, early on in my career, my peers and I were trained to have a wish list to take with us into negotiations. However, this was incorrectly only a list of what I wanted and not what the other party hoped to gain; in fact, I was once accused by a client of bringing him a 'shopping list'! Of course, I now realize he was completely right and that I had only been preparing for the things that I hoped to gain. So, make sure that, throughout your preparation, you think about what you can offer the other party. By giving someone something they want, they are likely to want to reciprocate and give something back. This shifts the balance of power.

IDENTIFYING THE OTHER PARTY'S NEGOTIATING STYLE

In order to fully understand what makes your counterpart tick, you need to try and identify their particular negotiating style. You can only achieve this by putting your emotions to one side and thinking objectively using the negotiating style framework described earlier in this book to guide you. If you do not know their negotiating style, be creative about how you can discern it. You will get valuable clues from the culture of the organization, other contacts you have in common, and people whom you know are in similar situations. If you have negotiated with them before, look back on previous scenarios to gain greater insight. Similarly, think about how they behaved and notice any cues that will give you an indication of how they will behave when you negotiate. For example, when I attended sales meetings with retailers, I trained myself to notice the signs when they wanted investment from us by spotting a change in their approach and pitch. It is vital that you use this knowledge as part of your preparation for the negotiation stage as it will help you feel on a level playing field.

PREPARING HOW TO RESPOND TO DIFFERENT NEGOTIATION STYLES

One of the main advantages of understanding your own negotiation style and that of your counterpart's is that you will be able to recognize how this will affect the relationship between you. For example, two people who are both confident and results driven could get on famously as they have a similar outlook, or they could clash horribly as both are direct and dominant. Whereas, if your counterpart values being popular and liked, they may say "yes" to your face when really they mean "no", which could slow down the momentum of the negotiations. Therefore, you should focus on trying to align your style with that of your counterpart. Gaining a clearer understanding of what motivates them will allow you to respond to them accordingly – but more about this in Part Three when I will show you how to use insight about styles in different situations.

3. BEING APPROPRIATELY AMBITIOUS

When it comes to preparing for a negotiation, it is essential to adopt the winning mindset as discussed in Part One. You need to be consciously ambitious throughout the negotiation process; at the start, in your win zone, and when you close. As author Maureen Dowd said, *"The minute you settle for less than you deserve, you get even less than you settled for."*

To be truly ambitious you must believe wholeheartedly in the value of what you are offering, otherwise you risk communicating self-doubt through your body language, tone and interactive style. This means being well prepared, with the facts at your fingertips, so you are ready to tackle any difficult questions or behaviours. Think of all the reasons why the other party will say "yes" and why the deal makes sense for their business. Remember, negotiation in its purest sense is about finding the win zone, where both parties can agree a mutually satisfying deal.

HOW TO SET YOUR AMBITION

To give yourself a good chance of securing the best outcome, you need to start the negotiations ahead of your ideal. For example, if you definitely need an extra two people to deliver a project on time, start by asking for three – this way you are far more likely to walk away with the two additional resources that you require.

Remember you are unlikely to get a "yes" to your opening offer – in fact, you need to retrain your brain and want them to say "no", otherwise you have not asked for enough. This is the first lesson in not negotiating with yourself: you need to challenge yourself throughout to be ambitious.

Before any negotiation, you should prepare your highest, high and low positions. You will automatically get a better result if you do not prepare for a "no" as the graph below illustrates. Contrary to popular belief, I maintain you should never prepare your walkway position as you are more likely to end up there if you do. For me, it is like a voice in my head – it softens my position, so I have trained my brain not to go there.

PREPARED POSITION

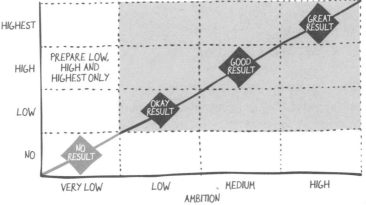

Instead, think of the low position as being at the bottom of your 'happy zone', with the highest as the highest believable position. Then apply this approach to every single variable of your proposal to increase your chances of securing the best possible outcome.

EXERCISE: HOW TO SET THE RIGHT LEVEL OF AMBITION

The holiday of a lifetime
10-day luxury holiday to the Caribbean
all inclusive, airport transfers, food
Special offer £8,000
Now only £6,500
Book now – only 1 room left!

Scenario: You have been tasked with booking a special holiday this year for your 20th wedding anniversary. Your departure dates are NOT flexible. You have both already booked the time off work and it must be a 10-day stay.

Things to remember: This is your partner's favourite destination. You have left it quite late to book and have already missed out on three good deals. Your time off is at the same time as the school holidays, so you know that availability of flights may be limited.

What would you be prepared to pay? Write down here what you would be willing to pay for the holiday:

_____

_____

_____

_____

THE ANSWER

The highest believable offer you should have in mind is £5,000 (after all, the holiday company seems keen to shift the holiday). Your first high offer should be £5,500 – as you do not know what mark-up the company makes on the holiday. Your lowest offer could be £6,000 – you understand it may be difficult to find another deal as attractive as this one, so you are prepared to pay £500 less than the discounted price if they negotiate hard.

The key piece of advice is to set your sights high as you are more likely to achieve a favourable outcome. A lot of people do not even try to negotiate because they focus on the fact the holiday has already been discounted. When, in fact, you should tell yourself that at worst, they may say "no" – in which case you can always refine your position. After all, you and your partner are going on the holiday, not the travel agent.

AMBITION AND CONFIDENCE DELIVER RESULTS

The main point of the holiday booking exercise is to show you the importance of challenging your own level of ambition. Above all, it is important to resist the urge to negotiate with yourself beforehand and, as negotiation expert, Carol Frohlinger says, **"Don't bargain yourself down before you get to the table."**

Keep reminding yourself that if they say "no", you can course-correct. If they say "yes", the deal works for them. By preparing your positions well beforehand, you will reap the reward of greater results, which will, in turn, fuel your ambition and boost your confidence.

This increase in confidence then kick-starts a positive cycle that leads to more ambitious thinking, which then generates even better results. This leaves you in no doubt that mastering the skills of ambition and confidence *will* have a direct impact on your sales and bottom-line profit.

4. AVOIDING WEAK SPEAK

One of the key ways of staying ambitious during negotiations is by avoiding weak speak – those phrases that weaken your negotiating position. So, to help you prepare before your next negotiation, here are some examples of what not to say when you negotiate, and the messages they convey to the other party.

You say:	The other party will think (either subconsciously or consciously):
"The best price at the moment"	I will come back another time.
"Ideally, I am looking to get"	You must be dreaming!
"My starting position is"	I wonder what's your finishing position?
"To be honest", or "Honestly"	Are you pulling the wool over my eyes?
"Our normal price is"	I am not normal so I want the special discounted price

Based on my negotiating experience, here are the five most common examples of weak speak and why you should *never* say them when you are negotiating.

1. *"Maybe we could meet in the middle"*

The art of negotiation relies on confident language. Thinking out loud can mean you come across as undecided and unclear and this will undoubtedly weaken your negotiating position. If you are not fully prepared before the negotiation takes place, you can easily end up hedging your bets and starting to compromise from the onset by using vague and hackneyed phrases such as, "Let's meet in the middle." If you think about your actual words, you are already offering to compromise, not to mention the fact that 'the middle' needs defining, too.

2. *"I do not agree"*

If you argue with logic you are more likely than not to end up in deadlock. Saying you do not agree will get you nowhere. You have to recognize that both of you have your own positions but at the same time understand that arguing is not negotiation. Take a step back and count to ten. Remember businessman and entrepreneur coach Brian Koslow's wise words: ***"During a negotiation, it would be wise not to take anything personally. If you leave the personalities out of it, you will be able to see the opportunities more objectively."***

3. *"Remember the benefits to the business are ..."*

One of the most common mistakes I have observed in negotiations is when people revert back to selling mode. Overselling can weaken your negotiating position. Always make sure you have finalized the selling process *before* you open the negotiations. In selling, justifying your position is a strong thing to do. In the negotiation, this actually weakens your position and potentially communicates that you really want this deal. Hold onto your self-control – that all-important building block of EQ.

4. *"That is my final offer"*

Whatever you do, try not to back yourself or others into a corner. Only say "that is my final offer" if you truly mean it and are prepared to follow through. Although it is often very tempting to respond with this remark, if either party has their back against the wall, it is unlikely you will arrive at a mutually satisfying conclusion. If later you concede on this position you will lose credibility – think of the story about the boy who cried wolf.

5. *"I will ask my boss"*

The other absolute negotiating no-no is saying, "I will talk to my boss." This not only undermines your own credibility, it also suggests you are not aligned as a team, which can allow the other side to force cracks. It is also an out-of-date and obvious tactic. In essence, you are telling the other party that you are not the decision maker. Even if this is the case, be careful not to communicate it, as it will weaken your negotiating position. Instead, draw on your self-reliance and your ability to make independent decisions. I am not suggesting you always need to go it alone – just use your EQ to control your emotions.

FOUR STEPS TO HELP YOU BANISH WEAK SPEAK

So, you now know how to spot the use of weak speak, and recognize that its use generally reveals a lack of negotiating confidence. Many of the phrases are, in fact, commonly used colloquialisms and you will probably start noticing them on a daily basis. But how do you start to get rid of it? The great news is that weak speak is easily remedied.

Follow the four steps below and you will start banishing it from your negotiation conversations, replacing it with confident language instead.

Step 1
You have been given the gift of awareness, so always notice when you and others use weak speak. A great way of doing this is to write down what people say when they weaken their position.

Step 2
Now start working on removing weak speak from your negotiations. When you notice that you are doing it, correct yourself immediately. For example, say: "I did not mean to say, 'I will pay you between £80 and £100', I actually meant to say that I will pay you £80." This is the think smart, act dumb technique – it is actually not dumb at all – as it clearly communicates that you are on the case and in control. Obviously, it is best not to use weak speak at all, but this technique will help you transition to using more confident language.

Step 3
People often use weak speak because they are thinking out loud and have not really planned what they are going to say. A great way to banish weak speak is to give yourself thinking time live in the moment. Do not be afraid to pause for thought. Remember, being steady and in control is better than saying the first thing that springs to mind. Think of yourself as responding not reacting.

Step 4
Finally, remember to ask for feedback from colleagues, family or friends. If you are going into a meeting with a colleague, get them

to spot any use of weak speak and let you know so you can make a conscious effort to avoid using it next time.

By working hard at using clear and precise language, you will immediately appear more confident and better able to influence the outcome of negotiations. People often ask me if they will appear arrogant if they remove weak speak. The answer is, absolutely not. You will come across as having courage, confidence and conviction. Remember people buy people. You are communicating with confidence and I believe this is what people buy.

5. PRACTICE MAKES PERFECT

According to the 10,000 Hour Rule, it takes 10,000 hours of 'deliberate practice' to become world-class in any field. This shows it is never too late to invest in yourself and your learning. Remember to role play with colleagues as part of your preparation before a negotiation and ask for any feedback. After your negotiation, make sure you reflect on what went well and what did not. Then use this feedback to set yourself new negotiating goals so you can keep raising your game. More about this in the final chapter of the book.

KEY TAKEAWAYS

You should now be left in little doubt about the importance of preparation in negotiation. Remember, if you fail to plan, you plan to fail, so make sure you take the following steps if you want to become a master negotiator:

- Understand and identify your own negotiation style so you know how this will impact your relationship with the other party.

- Understand what makes the other party tick by identifying their personal needs and drivers.
- Think objectively and identify your counterpart's negotiating style so you can prepare for different negotiating scenarios.
- Be appropriately ambitious before, during, and at the end of your negotiations.
- Prepare your highest, high and low positions. Do not prepare your walkaway position as you are more likely to end up there if you do.
- Master the art of ambition and confidence and you will achieve improved business results.
- Communicate your ambition throughout your negotiations by avoiding the use of weak speak.
- Speak in a clear and confident manner so you are better able to influence the outcome of the negotiations.
- Remember practice really does make perfect, so make a role-play plan and ask for feedback from colleagues, family and friends as part of your preparation.

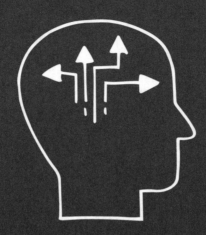

PART THREE

UNDERSTANDING DIFFERENT NEGOTIATING SITUATIONS

Now that you know how to develop your negotiating mindset, understand the importance of identifying your negotiating style and that of the other party, and have learned how to master the art of ambition and confidence, it is time to look at the different negotiation situations you may find yourself in.

Broadly speaking, there are three different negotiation situations: the win–lose negotiation, the win–win negotiation and the we–win negotiation. I will start with a brief overview of all three situations before breaking them down individually and giving you the tools and techniques to identify and respond to each situation in turn.

INTRODUCING THE THREE TYPES OF NEGOTIATION SITUATIONS

The win–lose negotiation

A great example of the win–lose negotiation is the famous scene from *Monty Python's Life of Brian*, in which Brian (played by Graham Chapman) is forced to haggle with a market vendor (played by Eric Idle) for a false beard while being chased by a troop of Roman soldiers. This type of bartering or bargaining is the most obvious form of win–lose negotiation. The only real variables at play are time or price. However, other less obvious examples are negotiating your salary for a new job or buying a house. Generally, these situations are short term – you really want an outcome and there is no relationship to speak of as you are unlikely to know the other party. This can make it more difficult to read the other party's behaviour. Furthermore, because most people want to be liked and do not want to appear too pushy – especially in the case of the British – they can often be under-ambitious in their request.

Although the win–lose negotiation situation can be appropriate for certain one-off scenarios, the real danger lies when people use it in ongoing relationships (often without even realizing they are doing it). Examples of this are when manufacturers enter win–lose negotiations with long-term suppliers by beating them down on price. They should be looking to move to a win–win situation in which both parties benefit from the negotiation.

The win–win negotiation

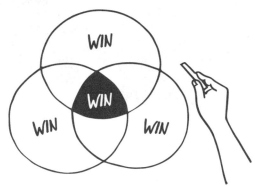

The win-win negotiation is always appropriate, regardless of the situation, although it is generally used when you are either in a business relationship with the other party or trying to build one. This negotiation situation is about finding an overlapping position that benefits both parties. For example, you could be negotiating with your new landlord for a flat – although achieving the best price for the rent is obviously important to you, you do not want it to be a win–lose situation as you want to build a tenant–landlord relationship with him or her going forward. If you pressurize the landlord into taking your highest believable offer (the lowest amount for the rent), you risk souring the relationship from the onset. No one likes to feel as though they have been conned. By moving the conversation to a win–win negotiation (perhaps by offering to sign an extended lease in return for not increasing the rent), the landlord is more likely to help you when you phone in the middle of the night to say your central heating has broken down. Furthermore, there is the added benefit of not having to move out so quickly.

The we–win negotiation

This is the rarest and most advanced type of negotiation situation because it cannot be achieved unless you have a long-term relationship with the other party *and* have highly developed negotiation skills. At the core of the we–win negotiation is trust. To understand exactly what I mean by this, look at the following equation, which breaks trust down into the following components:

$$TRUST = \frac{RELIABILITY + CREDIBILITY + EMPATHY}{SELF\text{-}INTEREST}$$

In other words, in order to build trust with another party you need to deliver on your promises (reliability), have the relevant experience and expertise (credibility), and be able to put yourself in the other party's shoes (empathy) while minimizing your own personal agenda (self-interest). If you are too focused on yourself, the level of trust between two parties automatically goes down. You need to want the other party to win – although the deal has to work for you as well.

An example of a we–win situation in business could be agreeing to provide the resources for the first half of a project, confident in the knowledge that the other party will provide the resources for the second half. This type of negotiation relies on both parties calling on their EQ, being optimistic, and looking for new opportunities that deliver a shared outcome. Great examples of we–win negotiations are Coca-Cola's joint venture initiatives with its bottling partners, and Dell and Intel's global alliance partnership in which each party needs the other one in order to be successful.

In summary, the majority of negotiation situations will start with win–lose until one person is brave enough to turn it into a win–win. Only when you have been able to keep the situation win–win can you aspire to take it to we–win together. The we–win together situation is the gold standard for negotiation and should be what you aspire to achieve whenever it is appropriate. It takes real experience and great negotiating skills from both sides, and for this reason is the rarest form of negotiation situation.

Now let's look at each situation in more detail, together with practical tools and advice to help you recognize and respond to the different situations.

DEEPENING YOUR UNDERSTANDING OF THE THREE TYPES OF NEGOTIATION SITUATIONS

Masterful negotiators can successfully negotiate in all types of situations, flexing their behaviours depending on their judgment of the situation and the behaviours being reflected by their counterpart.

1. THE WIN-LOSE NEGOTIATION

HOW TO RECOGNIZE IT

The first way to identify a win–lose negotiation is by noticing the use of power to control the negotiation (often used inappropriately). Second, win–lose negotiations are usually limited in their complexity as the variables are generally restricted to time or price. This limits the amount of preparation you can do, or need to do, as there are hardly any variables you can bring to the negotiation table. In fact, you could argue that the win–lose negotiation is not really about negotiating at all; it is about either getting or giving away concessions.

For many people the win–lose situation is the only type of negotiation they know. If they have demanded things in the past and got their own way, they are unlikely to do anything differently. Similarly, if you are holding the balance of power in a win-lose negotiation, you need to use your judgment to decide whether this approach is appropriate. For example, if you are negotiating with a new colleague over resources for a project and have exerted your power over them, you could either think of how to fool them, or imagine how your approach has made them feel. In all probability, they are likely to feel bitter and less likely to want to work with you in the future. Whereas, had you adopted a more collaborative approach, who knows what you would have received in return.

Sometimes, people unknowingly fall into a win–lose negotiation despite their best efforts to work collaboratively. One of the main reasons for this is lack of preparation. If you have not prepared enough variables to keep the negotiation moving forward, you can end up backing yourself into a corner by mistake to avoid losing face. You may then resort to the inappropriate use of power to achieve your desired outcome. So again, remember to use your judgment. In a business relationship, if you leave the other party powerless, they are unlikely to do their best work. In reality, you may have won the negotiation but you are more likely to lose on service, so take the time to think about the value that the negotiation achieved will bring in the long-term.

Finally, remember it is easier to spot the person who thumps their fist on the table to get their own way than it is to recognize the smiling assassin who stabs you in the back. This is especially true if you have let the other party exert their power over you for a long period of time. An example of this is when a client asks you to submit a proposal a few days before Christmas. You feel compelled to respond and work under pressure to deliver against the deadline, only to get an out of office reply when you submit it. This immediately causes resentment and irritation, and undermines the chance of establishing a balanced relationship going forward. It then becomes harder to change the negotiation style into win–win as someone must be brave enough to make the first move.

HOW TO RESPOND TO A WIN-LOSE NEGOTIATION

First and most importantly, you need to control your emotions. Remind yourself that you do not have to build a relationship to get the outcome you need. If you are an outgoing, people-orientated person who is drawn to relationships, you will find this difficult.

Whereas, if you are a task-focused person who likes to win at all costs, this will be easier for you to achieve. However, regardless of your negotiating style, you need to match what is in front of you and do what is appropriate for the situation.

Be aware that many win–lose negotiations result in an argument because of the lack of variables available. You may find yourself going round and round in circles as there is nothing else to bring to the table. Watch out for tactics and game play – it can be very unnerving if the other party belittles your points, bombards you with comparisons about the competition, or makes the negotiation personal. When you come across this in a win–lose negotiation, it is very easy for fight or flight to take hold. Do not be afraid to take time to gather yourself. Then follow these tips to help you respond effectively to a win–lose situation.

TIP 1. BEATING THE OTHER PARTY AT THEIR OWN GAME

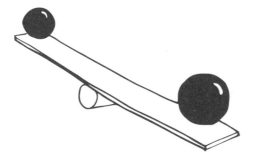

Although I would never advocate adopting a win–lose approach, in certain situations you may need to adopt this approach to establish or re-establish the balance of power. This could be in a one-off situation early in a relationship to establish power or as a way of rebalancing the playing field. For example, if you have agreed the commercial terms of a project with a client and they then change the scope, you may need to adopt the win–lose approach as a way of firing a warning shot across the bow to regain power.

TIP 2. ESTABLISH THE BALANCE OF POWER

It is important to remember that you only use the win–lose negotiation situation with caution. You need to know when you are doing it and be aware of the impact it has on the other person. How you use the win–lose approach is, in effect, the direct opposite of how you deal with it. You need to be direct and use positioning statements to give yourself the upper hand. Examples of these are, "Everybody else has said 'yes' to this"; "We're not asking for a lot"; or, "If we do not get this agreed, the whole project is in jeopardy." By prioritizing your own needs over theirs and being prepared to win come what may, you will shift the balance of power in your favour. This will ensure you are seen as a force to be reckoned with at the negotiating table.

2. THE WIN-WIN NEGOTIATION

HOW TO RECOGNIZE IT

The key way of identifying the win–win negotiation is by recognizing the role trading plays in it. As I have mentioned before, it is about finding an overlapping position for both parties, and this means both sides need to bring more variables to the table.

Most negotiation conversations begin with a win–lose situation, but the win–win negotiation enables both parties to move on from confrontation about time and price. If done properly, this can prevent you from giving concessions in order to get closure. This is not about relinquishing power – it is about taking a balanced approach, with both sides feeling like equals in the conversation. It is important to remember you cannot adopt a win–win approach on the fly, it takes both will and skill; you need to want to be like this and have the know-how to be able to achieve it.

HOW TO ADOPT A WIN-WIN APPROACH

The secret to adopting a win–win approach is keeping the end in mind and identifying the building blocks you will need in order to get there. Preparation is key – you need to prepare exactly what you want and what you are prepared to offer in return. This means writing a shopping list for you and for them. Bear in mind that some of the things you offer in return may be things you want them to say yes to anyway. For example, if you are negotiating with the other party over a new IT system, you may offer to train their employees as part of the deal. This offer could actually benefit you, too, as they are more likely to see the full value of the system you are selling. In other words, rather than offering the training for free, it is more beneficial to trade it in return for something you want.

Remember to prepare a different set of variables for yourself and for them. For example, one variable on your list may be the cost of your goods or services. Instead of preparing an amount to discount the cost by, it would be better to plan a different financial variable, such as the payment terms, to trade the cost against. This broadens the deal by bringing more overall value to the table. You then need to prepare with ambition. You should have your highest, high, and low position for each variable on your list and theirs. Remember to follow this principle: start with your high (which is the ideal) and then challenge yourself on what is the highest believable position. The low is the bottom of your happy zone. Next, double-check you are not negotiating with yourself before anchoring each variable in either time or price. For example, if you want them to agree to a three-year contract, state exactly when you want this to start.

Once you have finished your preparation, ask a friend, colleague or your boss to check it and make sure you haven't missed anything. The final part of your preparation is to anticipate any tactics or game play from the other side – it is important to identify any potential curve balls and work out how you can respond to them. More about this in the next chapter.

STEPS TO PREPARE FOR WIN-WIN NEGOTIATIONS

- Be clear on your desired outcome.
- Prepare your variables and their variables.
- Prepare many variables to bring to the table; the more you have, the more fruitful the negotiation will be.
- Plan your response to their tactics.
- Keep your ambition levels high during your preparation, taking care not to negotiate with yourself.
- Stay confident in your mind; if there is a negotiation conversation, in essence both sides have agreed they are interested.

HOW TO ACHIEVE A WIN-WIN NEGOTIATION

So, you've prepared for the win–win negotiation but how do you go about actually achieving it? Here are the three steps you need to follow to be successful in a win–win negotiation:

Step 1. Manage the mood

You need to draw on your EQ in order to manage the mood during the negotiation. Optimism and enthusiasm are contagious – so even if the other side becomes tactical, do not allow them to affect your mood. Instead, keep the mood appropriate for the deal to be done by being positive and keeping the negotiation conversations moving forward. This way, you are more likely to achieve negotiation success.

Step 2. Make your proposal

As part of the win–win negotiation, you need to stay confident when you make your proposal. A great way to do this is by trading your way to success in bite-sized chunks rather than trying to put all your eggs in one basket in the beginning. Remember, introducing new variables will help you maintain momentum and control the negotiations. Respond to their proposal with a relevant counter proposal but never concede for no return. Traditional negotiation training courses have often argued that you should *never* concede in a negotiation, but I believe this depends on your definition of a concession. In reality, in order to compromise, one party or the other needs to concede some of their variables if they want to get closure. The challenge is to pick the right variables to concede – which takes control, discipline, and the ability to think live in the moment.

Step 3. Keep track of the negotiations

This is particularly important in win–win negotiations in which there are a lot of different variables. A powerful way to keep track of the different variables is to give a verbal summary. This will help both you and the other party to summarize what has been discussed and agreed, what is being discussed and not agreed, and what you would like to discuss. Remember, in order to be articulate and convincing you need to take good notes. If the negotiation is very complicated, take someone with you and ask them to help you keep track by taking notes, too. Above all, do not be afraid to take your time.

3. THE WE-WIN NEGOTIATION

It is not surprising that I have left the most advanced negotiation situation until last. The we-win negotiation requires all of the negotiating skills learned from the win-lose and win-win situations and more, together with a genuine desire on behalf of both parties to work collaboratively. This winning combination of masterful negotiating skills and the ability to think ambitiously for both parties over the long term explains why the we-win situation is so rarely seen. Nevertheless, we should all strive to achieve it whenever appropriate, as it delivers the maximum value for both parties. So, it is important to know how to recognize it, how to prepare for this approach, and how to achieve this live in the negotiation conversation.

HOW TO RECOGNIZE IT

The three ingredients of the we-win situation are: a long-term relationship, high levels of trust, and a desire for both parties to win together. Equality, mutuality, and empowerment are, therefore, all important. This is particularly apparent when it comes to negotiating internally. If the departments within an organization have conflicting goals, self-interest is likely to be high and it is going to be difficult to achieve a we-win situation. However, in an organization where there is alignment across its different departments and they share a common goal, building a collaborative mindset will be easier.

A great example of the power of a we-win negotiation is to imagine you have been asked by your company to relocate internationally. It is a big ask as it means upping sticks and moving your partner and children to another country. The way in which the negotiation is handled will have a huge bearing on your working relationship going forward. If your boss treats the negotiation as a one-off deal (a win-lose situation), you will probably feel as though you are being forced to leave. However, if your company supports you in your relocation – practically, financially and emotionally – you are likely to view the move as an opportunity or promotion, and feel a greater sense of loyalty and enthusiasm for the job ahead. This will result in a better future for both parties longer term.

HOW TO ADOPT A WE-WIN APPROACH

Getting to we-win is about taking everything you have learned from win-win and upping your game. It is about dialling up your creativity and harnessing your EQ so you can be even more optimistic and opportunistic. The secret to achieving this is to stay open-minded, focus on the future rather than the past, and commit to building a strong relationship with the other party.

In order to put the relationship building blocks in place, both parties must be prepared to share information about their starting positions. This means being honest and open at the beginning of the negotiation, which is often easier said than done. If you think back to the relocation example, your boss or your human resources colleagues will need to ask you questions about your personal set-up and the commercials involved, and you will need to be honest in return, otherwise the deal will not work and inevitably trust will break down at some point. Both parties then need to think creatively about cost in the context of the long term. Care should be taken here not to share your aspiration. It is more important to clarify the exact starting positions for both sides. For example, the company needs to recognize that by transferring you to another country, they will save on recruitment costs. Furthermore, as you are familiar with the business, you are likely to hit the ground running and deliver immediate results, whereas a new employee would need time to get up to speed. This means that there are commercial benefits for both sides. Although hard to quantify, you need to place a value on these types of variables and then use them as part of the negotiation. It can be all too tempting to be economical with the truth or tell white lies at this point. Acting with principle and reflecting them back is easy to say but hard to do – especially when emotions are involved.

STEPS TO PREPARE FOR WE-WIN NEGOTIATIONS

- Prepare with an open mindset.
- Prepare questions that will open up the conversation and then use 'opening' questions throughout the negotiation.
- Think about the opportunity from their perspective, as well as your own.
- Prepare an appropriate starting position, which means being clear on the current situation.
- Plan longer-term variables, and then value and cost variables creatively and in a long-term context.
- Plan to share appropriate information, but this does not mean open-book costing.

HOW TO ACHIEVE A WE-WIN NEGOTIATION

I have already explained that achieving a we-win negotiation is no mean feat. It takes ambition, practice and hard work. Although most people want to trust the other party, it is entirely normal to have had our fingers burned at one time or another. This can make it even more difficult to build a we-win situation the next time around; after all, as the saying goes, once bitten, twice shy. So, to help you on your journey to we-win, follow these three steps below.

Step 1. Communicate effectively

Being able to communicate with energy and passion is essential in order to engage and influence the other party. In a we-win negotiation, you need to embrace the other party's good ideas and build on them. As with all negotiating situations, you need to keep your ambition levels high. However, with a we-win situation there is a particular focus on what you can achieve together in the future. You, therefore, have to ensure you have a buoyant and positive mood that enables you to brainstorm new opportunities with the other party and keeps the negotiation moving forwards.

Step 2. Build trust

Trust is all-important in the we-win negotiation so you have to ensure you expect and behave with principles before, during, and after the negotiation. This can sometimes be difficult to achieve; you need to retrain your brain to get out of self-interest mode and focus on winning together instead. It takes real courage to move the negotiation out of win-win to we-win but, if this trust is not reciprocated, expect it to revert back. Remember, if you tell lies, expect to get lies in return. Collaboration requires honesty from both sides – only then will you have the chance to build a true partnership.

Step 3. Be creative

Negativity is the enemy of creativity, so always go into a we-win situation with an optimistic mindset. Try to think creatively, live in the moment, and work out how you can turn the other party's responses into new creative variables to bring to the negotiating table. Make sure you look at the situation from the other party's point of view, as this will encourage you to think of new variables that benefit both parties. Finally, remember that positive people are more likely to bounce back from setbacks instead of giving up in the face of adversity. This ability to take the learnings from a situation and move forward is particularly valuable when you are trying to win together over the long term. This way you are more likely to find a mutually beneficial outcome.

SOME LAST WORDS OF ADVICE

I hope you now have a clearer understanding of how to identify and respond to different negotiation situations. Masterful negotiators have the ability to flex their style depending on the situation and person. In order to do this, you need to take what you have learned about your negotiating style and establish which of the situations you are going to find harder or easier to deal with. For example, if you have a leaning towards people and enjoy collaborating, it is likely you will find win-lose negotiation situations a challenge. So, to shore yourself up, spend more time preparing how you will handle their behaviour. However, if you are the sort of person who loves a debate, a challenge, or a bit of conflict, then the opposite is true and you will find win-win situations more challenging. In which case, take your time to prepare lots of different variables to bring to the negotiating table.

Finally, take the time to identify the types of negotiations that are the most commonplace in your day-to-day life. This way you can prioritize the situations you need to put the most effort into planning, doing and reviewing.

KEY TAKEAWAYS

I have covered a lot of ground in this chapter, so here is a recap of the main points:

- There are three different negotiation situations: win–lose, win–win and we–win.
- Most negotiations begin with win–lose, before moving to win–win, and, occasionally, to we–win together.
- The win–lose negotiation is characterized by the use of power. It is generally used in one-off scenarios and is limited to variables of time and price.
- On occasion, you may need to adopt the win–lose negotiation style to re-establish the balance of power.
- The win–win negotiation is characterized by trading. It is appropriate in all scenarios and is about finding an overlapping position that benefits both parties.
- To achieve win–win you need to manage the mood, prepare and introduce new variables, and keep track of the negotiations.

- The we-win situation is characterized by collaboration. It is appropriate when there is a long-term relationship with high levels of trust and a shared interest.
- To achieve we-win you need to communicate your ambition and commitment, build trust by being honest, and be creative so you can find new variables to bring to the table.
- Masterful negotiators are able to flex their style so they can respond appropriately to these different situations and individuals.
- To become a master negotiator, you need to recognize the negotiation situations you will find the most difficult based on your negotiating style.
- Focus on prioritizing your time so you plan, do and review the negotiation situations that are the most commonplace or challenging in your daily life.

PART FOUR

DEALING WITH NEGOTIATING GAMEPLAY

I have already touched on the use of negotiating gameplay in the previous chapter, particularly in regard to win-lose and we-win negotiations. However, based on my years of experience developing and delivering negotiation training, it is without doubt the area of negotiation that most people struggle with. For this reason, I believe negotiation gameplay is worthy of a chapter of its own. So, in this chapter, I will take you through how to recognize when the other side is playing games and give you the tools and techniques to deal with these tactics masterfully.

WHAT DOES NEGOTIATION GAMEPLAY MEAN?

I define gameplay as the unfair use of tactics designed to put you on the back foot and weaken your negotiating position. It is particularly prevalent in win-lose negotiations, when there is little interest in building a relationship with the other party. For example, you could be in a meeting where your counterpart is constantly checking their phone and avoiding eye contact as a way of establishing the balance of power. Some people may not even class this as gameplay. The use of tactics is generally more overt in a win-lose situation and can, in theory, be easier to spot and deal with. Where most people struggle to identify and handle gameplay is in a longer-term business context or where there is a relationship at stake. In these cases, the gameplay tends to be subtler and trickier to recognize.

GAMEPLAY IN BUSINESS

A common example of negotiation gameplay is arriving for an agreed meeting, only to be left waiting in reception for what feels like an unreasonable amount of time. There could, of course, be a valid explanation for the delay, so you have to use your judgment and ask yourself whether you would treat the other party this way. If the answer is no, then you are judging their behaviour to be unbalanced. It is highly likely that they are trying to remind you that they have the upper hand. Therefore, you need to call them on it or risk allowing them to establish a pattern of behaviour that undermines your negotiating position going forward. It is about rebalancing the playing field in your mind; ask yourself what the fallout would be if you did this. Then ask yourself why you are letting them behave in an unprofessional way towards you and the company you represent. Remind yourself that if you say nothing, you are in effect telling them that it is acceptable to treat you in this way.

Another common scenario in which it can be difficult to identify the use of negotiating gameplay is when precedents are used to get the upper hand. Perhaps you launched a product that did not deliver to expectations and your customer keeps using its poor performance against you in current negotiations. You need to remind yourself that you have remedied the problems with your previous product, and that the customer is aware that this is your Achilles heel and they are deliberately bringing it up time after time in order to soften your negotiating position. It is also worth remembering that no one can actually predict how the product will perform without the use of a highly polished crystal ball – there are just too many factors outside of everyone's control.

It becomes more difficult to spot their unfair negotiating tactics when they base their tactics on a modicum of truth. It can be tempting to take throwaway comments such as, "We haven't got enough budget,"; "We don't have the same R&D spend,"; and, "We are not the biggest in the market," at face value. After all, perhaps they have a point? However, if you do not recognize this use of gameplay, most people's natural reaction is to deal with it logically by giving a sensible counter argument, such as, "I understand your competitors are larger, however..." In this way, you may feel better by justifying your position, and the other party is likely to think that you have agreed with them, which means, in their mind, they have gained the higher ground.

1. HARNESSING YOUR EQ TO DEAL WITH GAMEPLAY

The examples above clearly show that handling negotiating gameplay is fraught with danger as misreading or ignoring it can unwittingly make the negotiation situation worse. Instead, you need to dial up your EQ by focusing on the four building blocks we examined in detail in the introduction.

- **Self-Awareness** – self-knowing and straightforwardness.
- **Self-Management** – self-control and self-confidence.
- **Social Skills** – relationship skills and empathy.
- **Ambition** – optimism and adaptability.

You need to draw on your self-awareness to judge whether you or your counterpart are unfairly using negotiating tactics to undermine the other party's position. You need to rely on your self-management to control your behaviour in the face of these tactics. By harnessing both your social skills and ambition, you will be able to diffuse the situation and keep the negotiations moving forward. After all, your over-riding goal is to reach a negotiation outcome that is acceptable to both parties rather than win a game of one-upmanship.

AWARENESS OF NEGOTIATING GAMEPLAY

A great tool to gain a clearer understanding of your relationship with yourself and with others, and how this affects the way you handle negotiating gameplay, is the Johari window.

	KNOWN TO SELF	NOT KNOWN TO SELF
KNOWN TO OTHERS	OPEN	BLIND SPOT
NOT KNOWN TO OTHERS	HIDDEN	UNKNOWN

The Johari window (Luft, 1969)

The OPEN box shows what is known to others and known to yourself. In this case, any negotiating gameplay is clearly out in the open. You should be aware that if you play games you should expect games back. An example of this would be two internal departments with conflicting agendas being difficult and inflexible and adopting a stance of 'my way or the highway'.

The HIDDEN box shows what is known to you but not known to others. These could be your personal fears or worries that you like to keep private. In these cases, attack can be the best form of defence. Here, the gameplay could be being liberal with the truth or procrastinating on making a decision in order to protect yourself.

The BLIND SPOT is what is known to others but not known to you. You may not even realize that you are playing games. Sometimes people describe these game players as smiling assassins. Perhaps you are pressurizing a colleague to meet a tight deadline or urging a supplier to cut costs. So, take a moment to reflect on your last negotiation and ask yourself if you played a tactical game. It is only by recognizing and stopping your own inadvertent use of gameplay that you can hope to become a master negotiator.

The UNKNOWN box is what is not known to yourself or to others. Perhaps you are negotiating with someone new for the first time. You will have to draw on your EQ to gain a deeper understanding of yourself and the other party, and their particular behaviours.

Due to their very nature, most negotiations will have an element of gameplay in them. The secret is having awareness to be able to recognize it, and confidence to be able to deal with it. Remember, if you do not balance the playing field, you are saying it is acceptable to be played, and, as with bullying, this could mean you are, unwittingly, encouraging them to do it even more.

The key to addressing gameplay is to ask yourself whether their behaviour is reasonable, and remembering that ignoring it is ceding ground to the other side. Equally, if *you* are playing games in negotiation, remind yourself that even if it seems harmless at the time, it could be undermining your credibility and breaking down the level of trust over the long term. Better to use your self-control and self-reliance to consciously decide what constitutes the appropriate behaviour that will enable the best outcome. After all, you expect to find child's play in the playground but not in the boardroom or in a business meeting.

2. RECOGNIZING THE MOST COMMON TACTICS

While we are on the subject of child's play, it is worth remembering that negotiating gameplay does not just happen in business. A great way of recognizing the most common types of negotiating tactics is to think about how your kids behave in order to try and get their own way. If you do not have kids, think back to the games you used to play when you were young and wanted to get your parents to agree with you. Nearly all of us grew up using unfair tactics to get our own way at one time or another. Whether it was stamping our feet if Mum or Dad did not buy us a packet of sweets or storming off to our bedroom when we were not allowed to go out with friends. I am sure you remember the occasions when you got away with it, and the times when you didn't.

So, take a moment to reflect on the last time your children demanded more pocket money or tried to make you feel guilty because they are the only one in their class without the latest phone. Think about how you responded to the demand and what you conceded in order to keep the peace. Now, see it through a business lens. How do you react in the corporate world if you present your proposal and are faced with a wall of silence? Are you caught unawares? Do you rush to fill the silence? Perhaps you feel compelled to improve your offer? Or do you immediately recognize it as the unfair use of tactics and treat it accordingly?

Below are the most common types of negotiating gameplay – both in the playground and in business.

THE MOST COMMON TYPES OF NEGOTIATING GAMEPLAY

1. Silence

This could take many forms. It could obviously be being quiet during a meeting, not responding to a proposal or ignoring emails. The other party's natural reaction to this would be to pick up the phone and ask for feedback and open the communication.

2. Physical intimidation

Physical intimidation can be one of the most daunting types of negotiation tactics to have to deal with. This could be the other party thumping their fist in anger on the desk, turning up to a meeting with five other people when you were expecting just them, or even giving you a smaller chair to sit on.

3. Time pressure

You have been given an unreasonable deadline to turn around a proposal. They know how long it should take you and are putting you under pressure on purpose. Another example could be threatening to walk away unless the deal is done then and there. Both tactics are designed to put you on the negotiating back foot.

4. Competitor comparisons
Everyone else does it better, faster, cheaper. Why should I recognize you? This tactic is generally designed to drive you to concede or match the either fake or real competition.

5. Too expensive
Another frequently used tactic is, "We do not have the budget." This, again, is generally used as a means to get the other party to reposition their offering.

6. I am not asking for much
This tactic is all about making a big thing seem like a little thing. For example, "I am *only* asking for a 5% discount," – this is, in fact, a big ask and should be treated as such.

7. Undermining you
This could be asking you to deal with someone more senior, questioning experience levels, or lodging a complaint and is generally an attempt to shift the balance of power in the other party's favour. It can be particularly difficult not to take this tactic personally.

The kneejerk reaction to all of these examples would be to try and justify your position. However, as we mentioned earlier, by justifying yourself in this way you are in effect accepting that they have a valid point. For example, if they argue your competitors offer superior products and you react by saying that research proves the contrary – you are reacting to their tactics with a data-driven counter argument rather than seeing them for what they really are. This will weaken your negotiating position as you are not acting or being treated like an equal. Master negotiators, on the other hand, would respond, not react, to negotiating gameplay.

3. RESPONDING TO THE USE OF TACTICS

Now that you are able to recognize the use of tactics, you need to dial up your EQ so that you can control yourself in the moment and respond in the right way. You will need to draw on your self-management skills to stay calm and process exactly what has been said, before deciding how to respond. Next, use your social skills and ambition to articulate your response in a way that does not back the other party into a corner, and establishes you as an equal. Remember gameplay is not negotiation – it is what gets in the way of finding an overlapping position that benefits both parties. Unfortunately, it happens frequently in business. It is, therefore, crucial to learn how to respond, not react, to tactics and remember that saying nothing is a sign of weakness. When carried out masterfully, this savvy formula will give you poise and control, which will help you boost your commercial confidence.

SOME ADVICE ON HOW TO RESPOND

First things first: ready yourself. Take a deep breath and take a moment to regain your composure. Do not feel pressured into reacting – instead, remove eye contact and give yourself time to order your thoughts and plan your response. Then follow my top tips on how to respond to the following negotiating tactics.

1. Silence

In my experience, the best response to the tactical use of silence is to treat it as a game and ask them, "Are you giving me the silent treatment?" It is important to use an appropriate tone when you say this so you can keep the mood of the negotiations upbeat. Remember, if the moods sinks, no one will want to do a deal.

2. Physical intimidation

Humour is a powerful way to diffuse physical intimidation. When six people arrive for your meeting, have the confidence to say, "Oh, I did not realize this was a committee meeting," or, "We didn't get the memo, can I phone a friend?" It is important to communicate that you know this is a tactic, but immediately move the conversation on.

3. Time pressure

The use of time pressure as a tactic can be a tricky one to call as, occasionally, this could be a genuine reason. However, if you have judged it to be gameplay, do not be afraid to name it. By saying, "You aren't going to get a better offer by putting me under pressure," you are showing that you know exactly what game they are playing.

4. Competitor comparisons

A good way to dispel the use of competitor comparisons is to mirror your counterpart by saying, "I could quote your competition back but I do not feel that is appropriate."

5. Too expensive

The 'too expensive' tactic is easily diffused with humour. An effective way to respond is by saying, "You cannot expect to get a Rolls Royce for the price of a smart car."

6. Undermining you

If the other party dismisses you by saying you are too young or inexperienced, respond by saying, "I will take that as a compliment – I am not as young as I look," and then move the conversation on. This way you are standing your ground and demonstrating that you should be seen as an equal at the negotiating table.

4. MOVING THE CONVERSATION ON

As you may have noticed, after each response to the tactics above, there was an immediate follow-up statement to keep the conversation moving forward. The key to keeping the conversation flowing is to draw on your self-confidence and self-control. It can be hard to spot gameplay as it arises in a conversation, meeting or negotiation. My advice is to anticipate and prepare ahead for any curve balls likely to come your way and predetermine your response to them. There is likely to be some degree of tactics in almost every negotiation you enter; when relationships are good, this can feel like banter, whereas if there is not a relationship, it can feel like harder work. However, you need to prepare in both cases, as in the case of negotiating gameplay, being forewarned really is being forearmed.

The table will help you do just that. Before your next negotiation, plan ahead by anticipating the verbatim comment you expect to receive. Close your eyes and imagine you can actually hear the other party saying it to you. This will help you to spot it during the actual negotiation conversation.

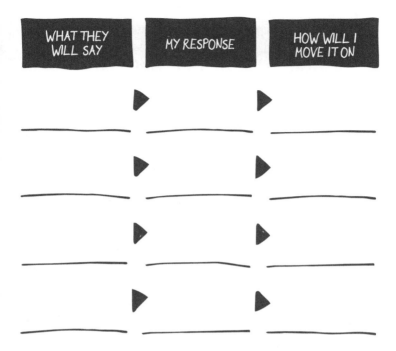

WHAT THEY WILL SAY	MY RESPONSE	HOW WILL I MOVE IT ON
	▶	▶
_____	_____	_____
	▶	▶
_____	_____	_____
	▶	▶
_____	_____	_____
	▶	▶
_____	_____	_____

The next step is to write down your response. Remember it should not be a logical or data-driven argument, but a way to level the playing field by naming the tactic. There is no right or wrong response – each will be situational and depend on the person, mood and relationship in question.

Finally, write down exactly what you will say to move the conversation on. Some people find it easier to articulate their response and move it on in one sentence. For example, if the tactic was, "I want to speak to your boss," you could respond by saying, "Maybe I should speak to your boss, but I do not think that will look good for either of us, so let us find a way of dealing with this ourselves."

Once you have completed the table, remember to prepare by rehearsing it out loud. Ask a colleague to play the role of the other party so you can practise how to respond. Above all, ensure you are using the appropriate body language and tone of voice to manage the mood throughout by asking your colleagues for feedback.

Although I have broken down the approach to dealing with tactics into bite-sized chunks, during negotiations it can be more effective to group the tactics together and make a call on the other party's overall behaviour rather than dealing with them one by one. An example of this could be, "This is getting us nowhere," or "It feels like we are wading through treacle."

5. GETTING BACK TO BUSINESS

Having readied yourself, named the tactic, and moved the conversation on, it is now time to get back to the business at hand – finding an overlapping position that benefits both parties. Make sure that you take control of the negotiations by helping the other party focus their mind. Make a new proposal or agree the next steps; both of these help to ensure that you keep the momentum.

Finally, after the negotiation, remember to adopt a best practice approach and reflect on what the other party said, what they did not say, which responses diffused the situation, and which riled them. If you find that they have taken umbrage to any of your responses, make a note so you can tone them down next time.

6. PUTTING IT ALL TOGETHER

Having examined the individual steps to help control negotiating gameplay, it is important to summarize the approach again. This will help build a clear picture of how each step links together to diffuse the unfair use of tactics.

FOUR STEPS TO CONTROL GAMEPLAY

Step 1: Ready yourself

- Use your self-control.
- Take a breath.
- Give yourself time to think.
- Do not react or feel the pressure.
- Remove eye contact.

Step 2: Call them on it – levelling the playing field

- Raise an eyebrow – you are not going to credit the comment with a response.
- Name what is happening – tell them they cannot pull the wool over your eyes.
- Treat it as a game – diffuse the situation while keeping the mood upbeat.
- Shame them – particularly if the other party is being unprofessional or rude.
- Hold a mirror up to them – beat them at their own game by responding in kind and dispelling their comments.

Step 3: Move it on – keep the conversation flowing
- We are both here to make money.
- Let us not be like this.
- I cannot give you something for nothing.
- How about we move forward like this ...

Step 4: Get back to business
- Make a new proposal.
- Keep the momentum.
- Agree the action plan or next steps.

Follow these four steps and ensure that you get back to business as seamlessly as possible, ensuring you are managing the mood throughout the conversation. This means controlling your body language and tone by keeping them situationally appropriate. Remember, if the mood dips, the negotiations are more likely to collapse and you are unlikely to achieve closure. By perfecting this process, you are well on your way to becoming a master negotiator.

FINALLY, REMEMBER TO CHALLENGE YOURSELF

When these methods for dealing with negotiating gameplay are discussed during training workshops, the common immediate reaction from most people is that they would never be brave enough to use these techniques. However, after a giant leap of faith, a great deal of practise and preparation, many report back that their new-found confidence has changed their negotiations for the better, forever.

Build up the courage to try these steps. Start by just spotting the gameplay and noting it down after the negotiation or meeting. The next step is to anticipate what they may say ahead of your next meeting and plan your response and how you will move it on. Even if you are not brave enough to respond live in the moment, just spotting the tactics and not countering them with logic will vastly improve the balance of power. So, with the words of motivational speaker Zig Ziglar singing in your ears, you do not have to be great to get started at this, but to be great you have to start!

KEY TAKEAWAYS

I hope that after reading this chapter, you now have the self-awareness to be able to spot the different negotiating tactics and the self-confidence and relevant techniques to help you dispel them.

Here's a quick refresher to help you on your way:

- Negotiating gameplay is the unfair use of tactics designed to put you on the back foot and weaken your negotiating position.
- People mistake gameplay as negotiation – when, in fact, it is the verbal ping-pong that gets in the way of building relationships.
- Gameplay occurs in nearly all negotiations, but is most overt in win–lose situations.
- Gameplay is used more subtly in win–win and we–win negotiations and therefore trickier to recognize.

- Harness your EQ in order to recognize and handle the unfair use of tactics.
- Use your EQ to help you decide what is appropriate behaviour for the situation.
- When you have judged the behaviour to be tactical, be brave enough to call the other party on it.
- By ignoring gameplay you are, in effect, communicating to the other party that it is acceptable to treat you this way.
- Remember to respond, not react, to gameplay – do not justify your position or you inadvertently give their comment credibility.
- When you respond to a tactic, it's crucial to manage the mood by moving the conversation on and getting back to business.
- Follow these four steps to control negotiations: ready yourself, call them on it, move it on, and get back to business.
- Do not overlook the importance of managing the mood; as soon as the mood dips, there is a greater chance of the negotiation collapsing.

PART FIVE

MANAGING THE NEGOTIATION CONVERSATION

It is now time to focus on that all-important moment when you draw on your negotiating mindset, and the confidence that comes from careful preparation, to come to the negotiating table and secure a positive outcome. A negotiation should be a conversation that is, by its very nature, a two-way thing. So how you converse with the other party is crucial to negotiation success.

If you are not able to articulate your proposal in a clear and persuasive manner, it is unlikely that you will convince the other party to agree with you. In order to become a master negotiator, you need to be able to manage the negotiation conversation with confidence. So, let us look at the different steps you can take to help you achieve this.

THE 7% RULE OF COMMUNICATION

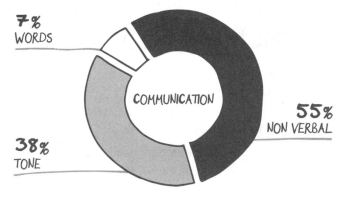

7%
WORDS

COMMUNICATION

55%
NON VERBAL

38%
TONE

According to research by scientist Albert Mehrabian,[1] only 7% of communication comes from the words we use, 38% comes from our tone of voice, and 55% from our body language. I would, however, challenge this breakdown in the commercial context and argue that all three components are equally important. In negotiations, what you say, how you say it, and the body language you use are all critical to negotiation success.

You do not need to be an expert in body language to understand how avoiding eye contact or crossing your arms when you feel under attack can undermine what you are saying. You have to believe in yourself in order to persuade the other party to believe in what you are offering. A great way to get back in touch with your inner confidence is to refer back to the confidence tool described earlier. This will help remind you why the other party is having a negotiation conversation with you in the first place and, most importantly, what you bring to the table. By silencing your inner chatter and feeling prepared for the negotiation conversation ahead, you are far more likely to walk the talk and appear assured, professional and full of commercial confidence.

1. PREPARING YOUR PROPOSALS

START WITH THE MOST IMPORTANT

First things first: I always recommend reminding yourself of exactly what you want to achieve from the negotiation conversation. This may sound obvious, but you would be amazed how many people lose sight of their goal as the negotiation progresses. So, take a few moments to clarify the desired outcome in your own mind.

The next step is to ask for the thing that is most important to you. You then need to judge whether this will be an open and shut negotiation or whether there will be further dialogue. For this reason, it is important to keep some variables in your back pocket so you can bring additional things to trade going forward. A rookie mistake is to put everything into your opening proposal, as this will leave you with very little room to negotiate. If your opening offer is rejected, you will have little choice but to concede. This means that you are unwittingly telling your counterpart that they can easily get concessions from you. If, on the other hand, you keep some variables aside, you will be able to bring them to the table later on to keep the conversation flowing. It is important to ensure that you come prepared with a game plan for which variables can be matched. Most people spend a lot of time preparing their opening proposal but fail to plan for what comes next and, as we said in Chapter Two, if you fail to plan, you plan to fail.

KEEP IT SIMPLE

The more complicated you make your proposal, the more difficult it is for the other party to process your offer and decide whether or not it works for them. Use clear language – remember, if you do not ask, you will not get. Be specific about what you want to achieve and what you are prepared to offer in return. This will help you avoid weak speak and/or making vague offers that can undermine your negotiating position. Instead, make your variables idiot-proof by anchoring them in reality. For example, be specific and ask for the exact date you want the contract to commence rather than just asking for the contract. A great way to make sure you keep matters simple is to have lots of small proposals rather than one lengthy one. This will help you manage the conversation and keep an accurate track of the different variables.

MAKE IT CONDITIONAL

The secret to making a successful proposal is planning it conditionally; in other words, you have to get to give, not give to get. A good way to explain conditionality is to think about negotiating with children. If you tell a child, "I will give you some chocolate if you tidy your room," the chances are they will just hear the word "chocolate" and won't even hear your condition. And, if your children are anything like mine, their understanding of tidying the room (hiding everything in their wardrobe) may be very different to yours. This clearly shows the importance of first explaining exactly what you want the other party to do to unlock the concession. So, remember, *every* time you prepare a proposal, make it conditional so it can't be open to interpretation and, at the same time, help your counterpart accept your proposal by spelling out exactly what is in it for them.

It is also useful to note that in commercial negotiations we are likely to be motivated by how we can benefit from a situation – whether it is a win-lose or win-win. So, make it easier for them to say yes by articulating the size of the prize. A good example of a conditional offer that achieves just this could be, "If you agree to the project scope, we will provide three project heads at £500 day rate and that will save you £75 in ongoing fees."

2. DELIVERING YOUR PROPOSAL

WHO GOES FIRST?

A frequent question I am asked is who should make the first move in a negotiation. The answer depends on the type of negotiation situation you find yourself in. In the one-off scenario – or if you think it is a win–lose situation – you should do everything you can to make the other person go first. Do not be shy; be direct and ask them to put a stake in the ground as this is the most effective way to identify their parameters for the negotiation. This information is gold dust – so try to tease it out of them if at all possible. Then listen carefully to what they say to ensure you have set the right level of ambition. However, if, despite your best efforts, they refuse to go first, you need to take the plunge or risk the negotiation stalling at the first hurdle. So be extreme in your offer and go for your highest believable position.

In the case of on-going negotiation scenarios, you should already know the other party and the business well. If you have done your homework, the parameters of the negotiation will be clear, so the emphasis should be on getting the conversation started. It is less important who goes when; the focus should be on being ambitious for both parties in a long-term context.

HOW TO OPEN WITH IMPACT

More often than not people tend to think out loud when they begin a negotiation conversation. People typically kick-off negotiations saying something along the lines of, "I am thinking that maybe we could proceed in this type of direction..." This instantly betrays their lack of preparation and confidence. A much stronger opening statement would be, "I am going to make you a proposal," followed by a pause (imagine a drumroll) to make sure the other party is ready to listen to what you have to say. This succinct and direct approach clearly shows the other party that you mean business.

As well as carefully selecting the words you use, you need to ensure your tone of voice is confident and not apologetic. Do not deliver your proposal as a question, say it as a statement and remember to take your time. It can be tempting to rush your proposal, when, in fact, it should be delivered at writing pace. This will help the other party process what you have to say and decide whether the offer works for them. It also enables them to take notes as you talk. Finally, make sure your body language is aligned with your words and tone: maintain eye contact and engage with the other party in a confident manner.

After you have delivered your proposal, have the self-control and presence of mind to stay quiet. Do not be tempted to fill the silence as you wait for your counterpart's response. I usually suggest waiting five seconds to allow them time to process your offer (any longer than this and you need to judge whether they are using silence as a tactic, in which case you need to call it).

3. TRADING EFFECTIVELY

Trading is the process of making proposals and counter proposals and it is the lifeblood of negotiation. It allows you to keep the momentum of the conversation moving forward so you can find an overlapping position that benefits both parties.

Master negotiators understand that to be truly skilled at trading you need to have the headspace to be able to listen live in the moment. You can only realistically prepare so much in advance, so you need to use your listening skills during the negotiation conversation to find out what else the other party wants from the deal.

LISTENING WITH EQ

People generally underestimate the level of effort required to listen attentively to the other party. Remember, hearing is involuntary, whereas listening is a skill. To help you improve your listening skills, it is worth taking a few moments to look at the different types of listening.

LEVELS OF LISTENING

As the diagram above shows, there are three levels of listening:

Level 1: Superficial listening

This is when you are pretending to hear what the other party is saying but are, in fact, thinking about something else entirely. Perhaps you are too focused on what you want to say next, or maybe you do not have the capacity to listen properly because you haven't prepared your own variables in advance.

Level 2: Selective listening

We are all guilty of only hearing what we want to hear at one time or another. For example, you may only listen to the variables you have prepared for but lack the ability to listen to new information. You, therefore, need to use your EQ to be more open-minded and develop your adaptability so you can take in the bigger picture.

Level 3: Attentive listening

This level requires drawing on your EQ to listen live and in the moment so you can process exactly what the other party is saying. It takes real effort and concentration and involves reading their body language and tone of voice, as well as the words they use, in order to get a thorough understanding of what they are communicating.

This capacity to listen attentively to the other party is key to being able to trade effectively and control the negotiation conversation.

4. BREAKING NEGOTIATION DEADLOCK

Trading is an invaluable tool for breaking negotiation deadlock as it allows both parties to introduce new variables to the table to broaden the deal. A lack of trading will generally lead to the '3 Ds' of negotiation: deadlock, disagreement and disappointment.

The first step to solving deadlock is to recognize when the negotiation is grinding to a halt. The mood might start to dip and the conversation may begin to feel like verbal ping-pong. Another sign that you might be approaching deadlock is if the negotiation conversation starts to become tactical. When one or other party begins to feel disappointed, they are more likely to use tactics to try and establish the balance of power. The secret to moving the conversation forward is to park whatever has caused the deadlock and accept that you will not be able to reach an agreement on this. You then need to remove the heat from the conversation by starting again with two different variables. By broadening the deal in this way and bringing new variables to the table, you are more likely to find common ground.

Another way trading can be used to break deadlock is to ask for an additional variable that allows you to make the concession. For example, if the other party has requested a discount of 5% in return for taking on your new product, you could make a counterproposal saying 5% is too high but if they put your product on display for four weeks, you will give them a discount of 3%. This offer will allow you to make a concession and resolve the deadlock. You know that featuring your new product in promotional space will drive consumer trial, which will boost sales and benefit both parties. By bringing more value to the table for both parties it becomes much easier to reach an agreement. The secret to broadening the deal in this way is making sure the variables are relevant to the conversation.

5. CLOSING
THE DEAL

At some point or other, you need to decide when to close down the negotiation so you can start implementing the outcome. This can sometimes involve deciding whether or not you need to fall on your sword. To achieve closure, one party or the other has to make a concession of some kind in order to agree the deal. So draw on your EQ and resist backing the other party into the corner. Be prepared to let your counterpart feel they have won but make sure that you have carefully chosen the variable you are prepared to concede. Remember, the most successful negotiations are win–win, so both parties need to feel as though they have benefited. Finally, before you leave the negotiating table, take the time to summarize the outcome so that both parties are clear on what has been agreed and what the next steps are.

6. NEGOTIATING VIA PHONE AND EMAIL

Negotiating face-to-face is, without doubt, the most effective form of negotiation so my top tip is to avoid negotiating via phone or email unless absolutely necessary. If you are working overseas, negotiating in person may not always be practical, but try and pick up the phone as a minimum. Negotiating by email is, without doubt, the most inefficient way to negotiate as it is difficult to convey your tone and manage the mood. It can also suggest that you are not confident enough to negotiate face-to-face or that the negotiation is not important enough to warrant a phone call. If needs must and email is your only means of negotiating, the principles above still apply; be specific and confident, use conditional trading, avoid weak speak and offer your highest believable position.

7. NEGOTIATING INTERNATIONALLY

The key to mastering the art of negotiating internationally is to recognize, respect and respond to cultural differences so that you can manage the negotiation conversation accordingly.

RECOGNIZING DIFFERENT COMMUNICATION STYLES

The first step to a successful international negotiation is to recognize your counterparts' communication style. The diagram is a useful tool to help you understand country-specific communication styles. Just by looking at it you can see that someone from Japan, who likes to avoid confrontation and is emotionally unexpressive, could find communicating with someone from Israel or France extremely challenging and vice versa.

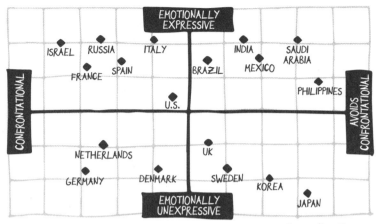

Source: Erin Meyer[2]

RESPECTING OTHER COMMUNICATION STYLES

Step two is to use your knowledge about your communication style and understand how this will impact a person from a different country. For example, an Italian who always wears their heart on their sleeve could appear overpowering to someone from Sweden who is more reserved and likes to keep their cards closer to their chest. It is only by gaining a clear understanding of your own particular communication style that you can respect how it affects others.

RESPONDING TO OTHER COMMUNICATION STYLES

Whether you are negotiating in the Netherlands or in the Philippines, you will be able to influence others most effectively by flexing your communication style in response to theirs. This does not mean you have to mirror your counterpart; instead, you should try to align your styles and gain a clearer understanding of what motivates them. So, when next you find yourself in negotiations with a highly expressive and emotional Mexican, do not let this faze you. Instead, stay calm and take the time to understand his or her particular needs and motivations so that you can respond accordingly.

Finally, although the differences in communication styles between countries can seem obvious and immense, do not underestimate the diverse nature of the communication styles among your colleagues in the office. People are reassuringly never the same, whether they live in Tokyo, Paris, Stockholm or London.

KEY TAKEAWAYS

I hope that this chapter has given you a clear understanding of the different ways you can manage the negotiation conversation to make sure you stay on the front foot and achieve your desired outcome. Here is a short summary of the key points that have been covered:

- Remember, people buy people – so communicate with confidence.
- Adopt a winning mindset and draw on your preparation.
- Walk the talk – your words, tone of voice and body language need to be aligned.
- Ask for your most important variable first.
- Keep your proposal simple so it is easy for your counterpart to decide whether or not it works for them.

- Make your proposal conditional – explain what the other party needs to do to unlock the concession.
- Open with confidence – be direct, not apologetic.
- Deliver your proposal at writing pace so the other party can process what you say.
- Make it easy for your counterpart to say yes by spelling out what is in it for them.
- Listen attentively to the other party to understand what else they want from the deal.
- Use trading to make proposals and counterproposals.
- Bring other variables to the table to broaden the deal and break deadlock.
- Keep the variables relevant to your negotiation conversation.
- Decide when you need to concede in order to reach closure.
- Recognize which variable you are prepared to concede and make sure it is not something important to you.
- Make sure both parties feel they have benefited from the outcome and create a win–win situation.
- Finish the negotiation session by summarizing the conversation and agreeing next steps.
- Try to negotiate face-to-face, at the minimum via the phone, and only by email when absolutely necessary.
- The key to negotiating internationally is to recognize, respect and respond to different communication styles.

PART SIX

CONTROLLING
THE
NEGOTIATIONS

I am often asked what is the most effective way to control negotiations to achieve the best possible outcome, and I always reply: if at all possible, do not do it alone. If you do have the luxury of additional resources, then take along a wingman who can act as your sounding board, and an extra pair of eyes and ears that offers a different perspective on the situation. Remember that during a negotiation the sum really is greater than the individual parts and this is particularly true in formal situations, such as when you are negotiating annual terms with a supplier or securing a new contract.

Negotiating as a team gives you another string to your bow. If you are a manager, it enables you to observe your team's performance live so that you can give constructive feedback to help them develop and improve. If you are the lead negotiator, it can give you much needed support. It is important to remember that you do not have to have a speaking part to make an impact on the negotiations – picture the court reporter in a court of law whose job it is to transcribe everything that is being said. The records made by this note-taker provide a factual report, something a court of law could not do without. Just having an additional person taking notes and tracking the negotiation can unsettle the other party. Perhaps more importantly, it also gives you extra bandwidth as a team to dial up your EQ and listen actively to the other party so you can read the meaning behind their words.

It is clearly important to make the most of the different negotiation roles available to you to help you find an overlapping position between the two parties. So, in this chapter we'll focus on the key roles in negotiations, how to ensure you are aligned as a team, and the invaluable role time outs can play in securing the best negotiation outcome.

1. IDENTIFYING THE THREE ROLES IN NEGOTIATION

There are three key roles in any negotiation:
the lead negotiator, the support and the counsel.
Let's now look at each of these parts in turn.

THE LEAD NEGOTIATOR

This person is the mouthpiece for the negotiation. He or she is responsible for pulling together most of the preparation, as well as for making the proposals and counterproposals (and almost everything that we discussed in the previous chapter). The lead negotiator should always be the main point of contact before, during, and after the negotiations.

THE SUPPORT

The support is sometimes mistakenly viewed as a junior role when, in fact, they play a powerful part in controlling the negotiations. The role of the support is to recognize the other party's behaviours, to observe how the lead negotiator's proposals are going down, and to ensure that the negotiations stay on track. The support should have the headspace to process everything that's happening in the negotiation – it is important that they draw on their EQ to interpret the meanings behind the words and relate it back to the situation in hand. They need to be able to read the other party's body language and feed this back to the lead negotiator to help them manage the negotiation conversation. Another key part of their role is to track the value of the deal, to suggest to the lead which variables to use to broaden the deal, and to ascertain the optimum time to close the negotiation. A great way to understand the role of the support is to imagine them as a 'lookout' keeping watch over the proceedings, and looking out for any signals that can help the lead negotiator steer a clear path through the negotiations.

THE COUNSEL

As the name suggests, the counsel should be a 'wise' person who can provide an objective perspective. Typically this role is taken by someone senior, however, it could be a colleague who is a strong facilitator. The role of the counsel is to help the lead negotiator get the deal done without getting too involved in the negotiation itself. It can, therefore, be a difficult part to play. The counsel needs to harness their EQ skills to draw on their self-control and self-awareness or they risk asserting their own views and undermining the lead negotiator as a consequence.

The overriding role of the counsel is to help control the negotiations by giving the lead negotiator feedback on what is or is not working. It is the counsel's responsibility to call time out if they notice that the mood is dipping and pour water on the fire if they feel the conversation is becoming too heated. Perhaps the other party is being tactical but the lead negotiator has failed to spot it; it would be the counsel's role to identify this use of tactics and, if necessary, give the lead negotiator advice on how to handle them. The counsel is also responsible for summarizing the negotiation conversation: outlining what has been discussed and agreed, what is being discussed and not agreed, and what still needs to be discussed. This ensures both parties are on the same page and helps keep the momentum of the negotiations moving forward.

It can be tempting, on occasions, for the lead negotiator and counsel to play the part of 'good cop, bad cop', but remember that this is tactical and if you play tactics you should expect tactics in return. Instead, the counsel needs to remind themselves that they are there to manage the mood and support the lead negotiator live in the moment. Finally, it is worth bearing in mind that it is a rare negotiation that has enough resources for all three roles. More often than not, the counsel plays a dual role, in which they also have to take on the 'support' role's responsibilities.

THE ROLE OF THE COUNSEL

DO	DO NOT
• Open with objectives and desired outcome	• Have direct involvement in making proposals
• Set the right tone and manage the mood	• Sit silently, observing
• Always support the lead	• Talk too much
• Spot deals	• Undermine or contradict the lead in front of the other side until the negotiation is finalized
• Call time outs	
• Summarize the deal regularly	
• Step in when the lead is struggling with tactics	

2. NEGOTIATING AS A TEAM

Having defined the three different roles and responsibilities in negotiations, the next step is to ensure these collaborate as a team. A great way to ensure that you negotiate together successfully is to adopt the plan, do and review principle.

PLAN

In my experience, some of the biggest negotiation blunders have come from a team who are technically on the same side, but have different priorities and understanding of their roles when they sit at the negotiating table.

So, first things first, it is critical that the lead negotiator brings the counsel and the support up to speed. It is not enough to ask a colleague to come with you to a meeting; you need to make sure they are prepared and clearly understand the part you want them to play. As lead negotiator, you will have done most of the preparation and will know the personalities and mindsets involved in the negotiations, so make sure you share this with your team. Let them know whether you want the situation to be win–win or we–win, and prepare for any curve balls that may come your way by telling them about any tactics the other party has used in previous negotiations. Do not be afraid to show your vulnerability to your team – if you know you often include weak speak in your proposals, ask your counsel to listen out for this and then let you know so you can make changes. Finally, remember to prepare signals that you can use in the negotiation to help you communicate with one another.

DO

This may sound obvious but make sure you physically sit together at the meeting so that you can work off the same preparation. You need to work together as a team throughout the negotiations, which means communicating regularly. All too often people see chatting to their team as a sign of weakness and apologize for it with, "Sorry can we just have a second." Do not be embarrassed – after all, why would you not talk to your team if it helps you negotiate in the best possible way? Remember to stick to your roles. If you are up against trained negotiators, they may try and force cracks between you. For example, they could try and sit you apart or eyeball the senior person in the team, in which case the counsel needs to use all their self-control to avoid responding and undermining the lead negotiator. If they do turn attention to your counsel, make sure the counsel on your team has the self-control to pass the baton back to the lead negotiator on your team.

REVIEW

After the negotiations, make sure that you take the time to review your ways of working. Ask yourself what worked well, what you would do differently, and what you have learned about negotiating that you can take forward to your next meeting. Make sure any feedback is constructive and focuses on the way you work together as a team.

A QUICK REMINDER

- Agree signals before the negotiation.
- Do not tread on each other's roles.
- Do not allow counterparts to force cracks.
- Sit next to each other so you can work as a team.
- Stay aligned until closure.

3. TAKING TIME OUT

I often refer to time out as the most underutilized negotiation tool there is. In my experience, people presume that taking time out will be seen as a sign of weakness when, in reality, it is incredibly beneficial to both parties to have a break from the negotiations. It is not surprising that master negotiators regularly use time outs to their own advantage to help them control the negotiations. Whether it is taking a break to have a cup of coffee or pausing the conversation so you can change the subject, time out allows you to take the heat out of the conversation and often presents a great opportunity to clear your head and identify some new variables to bring to the table. In the case of an ongoing relationship, it can also be used as a natural pause in the negotiations until your next meeting.

The secret to using time outs effectively is to do it confidently and without apologizing. We are used to thinking about time out in a negative way, so you need to reframe it in your mind into something positive. Remember, it is not about putting the other party on the naughty step – it is about giving you both the breathing space to bring new variables to the table. By saying, "I just need a few minutes to think this through," or "I need to make a phone call," you are buying yourself valuable thinking time, so use it wisely. Remember, if you called the time out, you need to be the one to leave the room so that you are in control of when you return to the negotiating table.

THE DIFFERENCE BETWEEN TAKING TIME OUT AND WALKING AWAY

People often confuse 'time out' with 'walking away' when, in fact, they are two very different strategies or tools. I generally say that people can't, won't, and don't walk away. In other words, people often threaten to walk away but rarely do it in a negotiation. The only real reason to walk away is actually to test the other person's limit, so I always recommend using it sparingly. Think of it as a last resort. It can be incredibly frustrating doing business with people who constantly threaten to walk away. Based on my experience, the main reason to use the threat of walking away is in a one-off situation when you want to check whether you have pushed the other person to the end of their win–zone. If they call you back, you know you haven't; if they do not, you know your proposal is not acceptable to them.

In the case of a win–win situation, I would only advise walking away when you have exhausted every variable. Make sure you only walk away at your low position (never your high) and avoid using any weak speak, such as, "This is my final offer," or "That's the best that I can do." Weak speak at this point can be seen as a chink in your armour, which can undermine your credibility and tempt the other party to push you one more time. You should walk away confidently (not reluctantly) as your body language needs to be congruent with the words you are using.

Once you have walked away, you need to draw on your EQ and recognize that if they did not agree to your proposal they may, in fact, have a better offer and you cannot win them all. Take confidence in the fact that it was the right time to walk away. You need to be emotionally resilient and bounce back from this setback by taking the learnings from the situation and reminding yourself that there will always be new opportunities with different clients or situations. Finally, make sure you are aligned within your organization. It is important that your colleagues support your decision or you risk having your credibility undermined should the other party try and force cracks between you by talking directly to your boss.

KEY TAKEAWAYS

I hope you now have a clear understanding about how working as a team can help you control the negotiations. By identifying the different negotiating roles, aligning as a team, and using time outs effectively, you will be well on your way to becoming a master negotiator.

Here is a quick recap to help you:

- Do not negotiate alone unless you really have to.
- Ask a colleague to act as your support/counsel and to offer an objective perspective.
- ·As lead negotiator, you are the mouthpiece of the negotiations and you will make the proposals and the counterproposals.
- As lead negotiator, you need to make sure your team is up to speed and prepared for the negotiations.
- As the support, you take notes and process what is happening so you can interpret the meaning behind the other party's words.

- As counsel, you are the facilitator who helps the lead negotiator get the deal done by managing the mood, spotting tactics, calling time outs, and summarizing.
- Negotiate as a team by adopting the principle of plan, do and review.
- Agree any signals to help you communicate prior to the negotiations.
- During the negotiations, sit next to one another so you can work together easily, look like a team, and communicate throughout the negotiations.
- Review your team's ways of working after the negotiation.
- Do not be afraid to call time out – it can be of benefit to both parties.
- Only use walk away sparingly to check whether the other party is at the end of their win zone.
- If you do walk away, be resilient – take the learnings from the situation and move on.

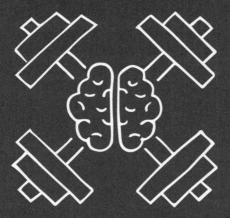

PART SEVEN

KEEPING
FIT FOR
NEGOTIATIONS

Now that you have reached the final chapter in *The Negotiation Book*, you have all the practical tools and techniques at your fingertips to help you master the art of negotiation. You should have a clear understanding of the important role EQ plays in helping you adopt a winning mindset, prepare for a successful outcome, understand the different negotiation situations, deal with negotiation gameplay, and manage and control the negotiation conversation.

However, it is important to remember that becoming a master negotiator does not just happen overnight. Just reading this book is not enough – the next stage on your journey is putting the theory into practice.

1. PUTTING IN THE HOURS

Negotiation skills are a set of commercial skills to live your life by. Just like playing an instrument or training for the marathon, they need daily practice if you want to be the very best that you can be. Think back to Chapter Two in which we talked about the 10,000 Hour Rule. It takes 10,000 hours of 'deliberate practice' to become world class in any field, so do not save your preparation for your big business negotiations, weave it into your everyday life.

A great way to do this it to think about all the tasks you do in a week, then ask yourself what practical steps you can take for a better outcome from your emails, meetings and interactions with people. Do not just limit yourself to workplace scenarios; it could be negotiating with your partner over who's turn it is to take the bins out or debating with your children about what time they should go to bed. You will be surprised by how many negotiation opportunities take place every day that give you the chance to put the theory into practice.

So, next time you are asked to agree to something, make sure you think about what you want in return for saying yes. Or, if you are the person doing the asking, remember to plan for what happens if the other party says no. After all, negotiation is like a muscle; the more you practise, the stronger and more powerful the muscle will get.

THREE PRACTICAL STEPS TO HELP YOU GET FIT FOR YOUR NEGOTIATIONS

An article in the *Harvard Business Review* by Katzenbach, Steffen and Kronley,[3] pointed out that, ***"People will change their behaviour if they see the new behaviour as easy, rewarding and normal."*** I am a big believer in this approach, which is why I have worked hard to make sure the tools and techniques in this book are accessible and easy to apply in real life.

So, follow the three steps below to help you change your behaviour and bring your negotiation skills to life.

MAKE IT EASY
- Pick one area to improve and then master it – for example, being more ambitious, or eliminating weak speak.
- Remember, it's not rocket science; use the practical tools and techniques in this book to help you.
- Tell yourself, "I have the skills and knowledge to do this" – the only barrier to success is not putting in the effort.

- You may already be doing some of this, so do not overlook the skills and strengths you already have.

MAKE IT REWARDING
- Recognize that this behaviour will give you results (emotionally or practically) that are valuable to you.
- Adopt the principle of plan, do and review so that you see all of the benefits.
- Put mechanisms in place to reward this behaviour and provide incentives.
- Understand that the more effort you put in, the more you will get out of it.

MAKE IT NORMAL
- Weave the changes into your everyday life.
- Make it a habit, for example, every time you go to a meeting, think about how you will prepare.
- Use common language to help you communicate effectively.
- Share best practice among the people you work closely with.

2. GETTING FEEDBACK

In the words of author and business guru Ken Blanchard, *"Feedback is the breakfast of champions."* And just as world-class athletes spend hours with their coaches analysing their play so they can up their game, master negotiators actively seek out feedback to help them change their behaviour so they can keep raising the bar.

Feedback can be from yourself – what do you think went well in the negotiation, what areas do you believe you need to improve on? Or it could be feedback from a colleague – perhaps your counsel – on how you controlled the negotiations. Did you use weak speak during your proposals? Did you handle the other party's tactics effectively? Or, it could be formal feedback from your boss as part of your annual review. In all of these situations, it is crucial to put the feedback in context and take the emotion out of it, by dealing with the facts. Remind yourself that constructive feedback is an invaluable tool to help you improve your negotiation performance. Delivered well, feedback will boost your motivation and confidence levels and help you to notice any blind spots (think back to the Johari window on page 70) so you can further develop your negotiation skills.

Once you have been given feedback, the secret is to act on it by adopting the principle of plan, do and review. Listen carefully to what has been said and think about what you could do differently. For example, if the feedback was that you were not ambitious enough in your ask, take the time to understand why you talked yourself down. Then plan what you could do next time to boost your confidence so that you enter the negotiations armed with your highest believable offer.

Above all, do not bury your head in the sand and blindly carry on doing what you did before. By ignoring constructive feedback you risk getting stuck in a negotiation rut. As Einstein said, the definition of insanity is "doing the same thing over and over again and expecting different results."

3. MEASURING YOUR PERFORMANCE

I firmly believe that tracking your performance is the key to keeping fit for negotiations. After all, if you cannot measure it, you cannot manage it. By proactively measuring your progression, you will boost your motivation levels and unlock your full potential so you can achieve real negotiation success.

The table below will help you measure your negotiation performance by focusing on the following key areas:

- What have I mastered and what are my examples?
- What do I need to start and stop?
- When will the negotiation situations arise?
- Who can help me achieve my goals?

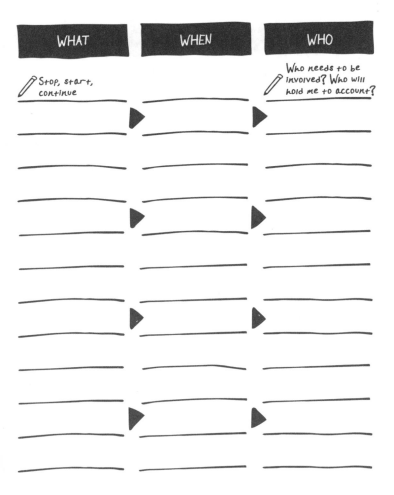

WHAT	WHEN	WHO
Stop, start, continue		Who needs to be involved? Who will hold me to account?

This is your commercial fitness plan and as you begin to fill it in, bear in mind that you are focusing on your behaviours and *how* you performed in the negotiation, as well as the result itself. The actual outcome may be out of your control, however, you could still have performed to the best of your ability.

4. RAISING THE BAR

One of the key attributes that all successful people share is the belief that good is not good enough. This is particularly true of Olympic athletes who aspire to greatness, constantly upping their game so they can beat their personal best. Double Olympic cycling champion, Victoria Pendleton, set herself a new and demanding challenge when she retired from cycling and retrained to become a jockey. She came fifth at Cheltenham in 2016 and described it as "probably the greatest achievement of my life". This clearly shows the incredible power of a growth mindset and how this enables you to reach the pinnacle of success.

A powerful way to help you up your negotiation game is to ask yourself these four masterful questions *before* each negotiation:

1. WHY SHOULD I FEEL CONFIDENT?
Refer back to the confident mindset tool on page 13 and write down all the reasons why you should feel confident about going into the negotiations.

2. WHAT WILL THEIR TACTICS BE?
Prepare ahead for any curve balls that may come your way by filling in the table on page 79, writing down the tactic, your response, and how to move the conversation on.

3. WHAT IS MY AMBITIOUS OPENER?

Make sure you open ambitiously by preparing your highest, high and low position as outlined in the graph on page 29.

4. HOW WILL I BREAK DEADLOCK?

Boost your confidence by preparing different variables to bring to the table in case you need to broaden the deal.

By taking the time to answer these four questions you will be enabling yourself to perform to the best of your ability.

My final piece of advice is to take inspiration from those around you who stand out from the competition, regardless of their field of excellence. By believing in yourself and setting new and challenging negotiating goals, you, too, can unlock your commercial confidence, drive your performance, and become a true master negotiator. I will sign off now by leaving you with the inspiring words of the late Muhammad Ali:

"Champions aren't made in gyms. Champions are made from something they have deep inside them – a desire, a dream, a vision. They have to have last-minute stamina, they have to be a little faster, they have to have the skill and the will. But the will must be stronger than the skill."

KEY TAKEAWAYS

As you continue on your journey to becoming a master negotiator, here's a final reminder of how to put the negotiation theory into practice:

- Negotiation skills require daily practice – think about all the opportunities during the week when you can practice negotiating, whether it's with family, friends or at work.
- Make negotiation EASY, REWARDING and NORMAL as a way of embedding new learning and changing behaviours.
- Feedback is the breakfast of champions – ask friends and colleagues for feedback on your performance so you can keep raising the bar.
- Listen carefully to feedback, then adopt the principle of plan, do and review so you can keep improving your negotiation skills.
- Keep fit for negotiation by tracking your performance – after all, if you can't measure it, you can't manage it.
- Keep a record of what you have mastered, what you need to start or stop, when you have used your skills, and who can help your reach your goal.
- Know the answers to the four masterful questions for every negotiation conversation.
- Believe in yourself and keep raising the bar by continuing to set new and challenging negotiation goals.

FURTHER READING

- *Drive: The Surprising Truth About What Motivates Us*, Daniel Pink, 2011
- *Eat That Frog – 21 Great Ways To Stop Procrastinating And Get More Done In Less Time*, Brian Tracy, 2007
- *Emotional Capitalists: The Ultimate Guide For Developing Emotional Intelligence For Leaders*, Dr Marytn Newman, 2014
- *Emotional Intelligence: Why It Can Matter More Than IQ*, Dan Goleman, 1996
- *Getting To Yes: Negotiating An Agreement Without Giving In*, Roger Fish, William Ury 2012
- *How To Win Friends And Influence People*, Dale Carnegie, 2006
- *In Business As In Life – You Don't Get What You Deserve, You Get What You Negotiate*, Chester L. Karrass, 1999
- *7 Habits Of Highly Effective People*, Stephen Covey, 2004
- *Start With The Why: How Great Leaders Inspire Everyone To Take Action*, Simon Sinkek, 2011
- *The Effective Executive*, Peter Drucker, 2007
- *The Chimp Paradox*, Steve Peters, 2012
- *The Mindfulness Book: Practical Ways To Lead A More Mindful Life"*, Dr Martyn Newman, 2016
- *Time To Think – Listening To Ignite The Human Mind*, Nancy Kline, 2002
- *To Sell Is Human*, Daniel Pink, 2014
- *Who Moved My Cheese?* Spencer Johnson, 1999
- *Women Don't Ask*, Linda Babcock, Sara Laschever, 2007
- *Working With Emotional Intelligence*, Dan Goleman, 1999

REFERENCES

[1]   Albert Mehrabian. *Silent Messages: Implicit Communication of Emotions and Attitudes*. 2nd ed. Belmont, Calif.: Wadsworth Pub. Co., 1981.

[2]   Erin Mayer, *Getting to si, ja, oui, hai, and da*. Harvard Business Review, December 2015

[3]   Jon Katzenbach, Llona Steffen and Caroline Kronley, "Cultural Change That Sticks: Start with What's Already Working." Harvard Business Review, Harvard Business School Publishing, July-Aug 2012

ACKNOWLEDGEMENTS

This book would not have been possible without the help of the hundreds of customers, clients and colleagues who have given me countless opportunities over the last 25 years to hone my negotiation expertise. I would particularly like to thank Dr Martyn Newman for opening my eyes to the power of emotional intelligence. It was meeting Martyn and being trained by him as an EQ practitioner that has enabled me to develop commercial training and coaching programmes interwoven with EQ principles that deliver real impact in the business world.

Thanks to my amazing family: my husband James and my daughters Talya and Amelie who keep me on my toes by helping me put my negotiation skills to the test on a regular basis! One of the key reasons behind my decision to write this book was to inspire my daughters to become strong individuals who can compete on an equal footing by having confident commercial conversations whatever the situation.

A special mention needs to go to my parents for their unfailing support – Dad for being a fantastic grammatical sounding board and wise old business sage, and Mum for her invaluable help sense checking this book.

Thanks to my team at Diadem for their energy, passion and commitment, in particular Katharine Wijsman, who helped to keep me on track as I wrote this book.

Finally, thanks to Martin Liu, Niki Mullin and Sara Taheri at LID Publishing who first suggested writing a book on negotiation and helped ensure the whole process was as seamless as possible.

ABOUT THE AUTHOR

NICOLE SOAMES is a highly qualified coach and EQ practitioner with extensive commercial experience gained from 12 years of leveraging large sales teams for Unilever and United Biscuits, followed by 13 years spent developing and delivering training programmes across the globe. In 2009, Nicole founded Diadem, the leading commercial skills training and coaching company. With over 85 clients in more than 15 countries, Diadem has helped many thousands of people become commercial athletes in negotiation, selling and influencing, account management, marketing, presenting, strategy, coaching, and leadership and management.

Follow Nicole on Twitter **@nicolediadem**
Or visit the website **www.diademperformance.com**

Contact Nicole for advice, training or speaking opportunities :
nicole.soames@diademperformance.com

Visit **www.thenegotiationbook.com** to download audio files to help you on your journey to becoming a master negotiator.